T0038915

MASTERS AT WORK

ALSO AVAILABLE

MASTERS AT WORK

BECOMING AN EVENT PLANNER

ARMAND LIMNANDER

SIMON & SCHUSTER

New York   London   Toronto   Sydney   New Delhi

Simon & Schuster
1230 Avenue of the Americas
New York, NY 10020

Copyright © 2021 by Simon & Schuster, Inc.

First Simon & Schuster hardcover edition January 2021

SIMON & SCHUSTER and colophon are registered trademarks of
Simon & Schuster, Inc.

For information about special discounts for bulk purchases, please contact
Simon & Schuster Special Sales at 1-866-506-1949 or
business@simonandschuster.com.

The Simon & Schuster Speakers Bureau can bring authors to your live event. For
more information or to book an event, contact the Simon & Schuster Speakers
Bureau at 1-866-248-3049 or visit our website at www.simonspeakers.com.

Manufactured in the United States of America

1   3   5   7   9   10   8   6   4   2

Library of Congress Cataloging-in-Publication Data has been applied for.

ISBN 978-1-9821-4042-7
ISBN 978-1-9821-4043-4 (ebook)

To Marina and Gérald

CONTENTS

INTRODUCTION

hree Hundred Vesey is an anodyne building plonked down in Battery Park City, the soporific neighborhood in New York that was partly created with landfill from the World Trade Center excavation site in the early 1970s. Across the street there is a luxury mall that always seems to be empty; beyond it is the eight-lane West Side Highway, and just past that looms the Freedom Tower, the hulking monolith that replaced the original World Trade Center with a surfeit of office space but none of the original towers' spindly elegance or architectural integrity. There is a daily barrage of tourists visiting the 9/11 Memorial, and it's hard to shake off a feeling of dread thanks to the permanent police barricades. In other words, it's not a place that New Yorkers would consider even remotely cool.

And yet, on a misty fall evening in October 2019, a cavalcade of black cars converged precisely on that spot, depositing a motley crew of partygoers who were clearly not in their natural habitat. Women in shimmering dresses and men sporting conversation-worthy haircuts breezed past the corporate lobby where thousands of suits swipe access cards day in and day out in order to do what one can only assume is very important work. The building was deserted after hours, so these atypical visitors were quickly whisked up in elevators to the third floor. As soon as the doors opened they entered a different universe.

There was no office furniture—or furniture of any kind, or even corridors, for that matter. Instead, people filed into a serpentine tunnel that was completely dark save for strategically positioned arches of blue and pink LED lights marking the way forward, until it opened up into an enormous black room with forty-foot ceilings. At the far end was a white Plexiglas bar that glowed, beckoning as if a UFO had chosen to alight there with the sole purpose of plying humanity with vodka. Large hexagonal neon structures set against the long wall leading to it cast a cool blue glow.

So far, so sci-fi; but there were also lush plants, twinkling votive candles, and comfortable seating areas to bring everyone back to earth. The space felt imposing but welcoming, an important balance to strike. This was, after all, not a movie set but a charity event—specifically, the Creative Time Gala, a yearly highlight of the New York art world. A nonprofit arts organization supporting the creation of large-scale, socially engaged public artworks, Creative Time has operated since 1974, collaborating with the likes of Takashi Murakami, Kara Walker, and Felix Gonzalez-Torres, among many others. On this occasion, the honoree was Jenny Holzer, the neo-conceptual American artist best known for her astringent aphorisms ("Abuse of Power Comes as No Surprise"; "Protect Me from What I Want"; "Expiring for Love Is Beautiful but Stupid"), which are often displayed in public spaces like billboards or projected onto buildings. Illuminated electronic displays that run her sentences like ticker tape are also an important and well-known part of her practice—thus the LED-lighting motif that prevailed.

Guests milled about admiring the decor and one another, occasionally pausing to combine the two by taking selfies next to a strategically placed Creative Time neon sign by the entrance. After cocktails and snacks (tiny quail eggs topped with even tinier fish eggs!), heavy curtains that formed a black wall were drawn, revealing the room where the main event was being held. Trustees of every major New York City museum, gallerists, collectors, film director Sofia Coppola, actors Benedict Cumberbatch and Rachel Weisz, music impresario Mark Ronson, and close to 350 other revelers followed Holzer and Creative Time executive director Justine Ludwig, weaving between tables of different sizes and shapes scattered around large trees that formed a leafy canopy. Guests were soon seated and bantering; a battalion of waiters served them as Holzer received her award and Ludwig gave her speech. An hour or two later, after all was said and done, everyone returned to the bar area, which was now the setting for a dance party. Black lights were activated, and reactive tape that had been deployed throughout the venue lit up in Day-Glo colors. The last of the extremely content guests stumbled out in the wee hours.

By the following afternoon, there was absolutely no evidence of the carousing that had taken place. Like a colony of single-minded ants, scores of movers swooped in at nine a.m. and dismantled the mise-en-scène in what seemed like minutes. Every single thing in the room, from the stage and lights down to the napkins and forks, was carried off and placed in trucks. When they were done, what had been a memorable locale resembled a vast, abandoned stock-trading pit—which is, in fact, what it actually was.

Lest you think that this evening came together as naturally as it felt, consider some of what was required to make it happen:

- 34 dinner tables
- 340 table settings

- 340 chairs
- One 40-foot long bar
- One 12-foot long bar
- 40 large potted plants
- Eight 30-foot tall trees
- 100 bushels of tree branches
- 400 candles and candleholders
- 150 theatrical lights
- 8 LED arches
- 1,500 feet of LED rope lighting
- 175 feet of mirrored surfaces
- 600 feet of black drapery
- 12 feet of faux wall
- One custom-made neon sign
- 60 waiters
- 16 trucks over the course of three days
- 70 movers
- One Temporary Place of Assembly Certificate of Operation permit from New York City

The person responsible for ensuring that all of these elements came together seamlessly, at the right time, under the best possible conditions, and without a hitch was Bronson van Wyck. He is an event planner.

CHAPTER ONE

Extravagant though it may seem, the Creative Time benefit was only one of hundreds of such bashes that van Wyck (rhymes with "bike") has produced as a matter of course—and it was by no means a particularly demanding or complicated one. In New York, where he is based, there is never a shortage of parties. His twin companies—Van Wyck & Van Wyck, which specializes in personal events, and Workshop, which focuses on corporate clients—are undisputed leaders in the event planning field. Van Wyck is known for his no-holds-barred approach to entertaining, at home and abroad, and over the past twenty years he has developed a client list that includes brands like Mercedes-Benz, Estée Lauder, Cartier, Chanel, ABC Television Network, Deutsche Bank, Samsung, Amazon, J.Crew, Condé Nast, Goop, Dom Pérignon, and Ritz-Carlton Hotels, to name but a few. On the private side there are Presidents Obama, Bush, and Clinton; Alicia Keys and Swizz Beatz; Gwyneth Paltrow; Katy Perry;

Beyoncé Knowles; Rupert Murdoch; Madonna; George Lucas; Calvin Klein; and the queen of Jordan. Keep in mind that there are many others who prefer to remain anonymous, and even more who are not bold-faced names.

Van Wyck amassed this roster over the past twenty years as the event planning business grew exponentially. David Adler, the chairman and founder of *BizBash*, a leading trade publication in the field, estimates that in the United States today, there are between 4,000 and 6,000 professional event planners—this does not include, of course, all the assistants at companies big and small that wind up organizing office Christmas parties or morale-building retreats. Events bring in about $6 billion a year just in New York City, where there are some 2,400 party venues. Adler describes the industry as a pyramid, with its base made up of concerts, festivals, and sporting events. Above that comes business entertaining— for example, when executives take out a group of associates to a fancy restaurant on an expense account in order to close a deal. Next up are corporate sales meetings, product launches, and conferences. Finally, at the apex, is experiential event design, which is what van Wyck and a select few others do.

Top event planners operate as lifestyle consultants as

much as anything else. They have perfected the art of socializing and allow people to feel their best in order to spark connections. Using design, food, and entertaining, they transport guests to carefully conceived, often fantastical temporary spaces in which everyone can drop their inhibitions and comfortably interact on a level playing field. For this, van Wyck and his peers can command impressive budgets: it's not uncommon for them to produce events with price tags ranging from $1,000 to $10,000 a head.

If you think van Wyck's job is all about party hopping with fabulous people, though, you're in for a rough surprise. His life sounds glamorous, but the reality of putting together a spectacular soirée is anything but. Though the big ideas are fun and creative and personality-driven, making them a reality requires a daily—if not hourly— grind. Event planning is a service-driven profession in which self-abnegation, adaptability, and flexibility are essential survival traits. When a client requests changes at the very last second, an event planner can't afford to be flustered, disappointed, or frustrated. He simply has to make them.

Van Wyck founded the company in 1999 with his mother, Mary Lynn, who still works with him and shuttles back and forth between New York and her home in Arkansas. His sister, Mimi, joined a couple of years later and currently oversees a Van Wyck & Van Wyck outpost in Charleston. Between his Manhattan headquarters, Mimi's office in South Carolina, and a 33,000-square-foot warehouse he keeps in New Jersey, van Wyck employs a full-time staff of about fifty, roughly divided into three teams. Project managers and coordinators are responsible for client interface and guest relations; designers oversee interior architecture, sets, and lighting; producers take care of carpentry, soft furnishings, scenic paintings, flowers, permits, and plans. On the Workshop side, there is also a digital content group, as well as talent bookers for event performances.

Several weeks before the Creative Time Gala, van Wyck invited me to sit in on a call with "the client." He has worked with several other not-for-profit organizations in the past, but this was his first experience with Creative Time. A board member with whom van Wyck had collaborated on private events had asked him to take on the gig. Van Wyck's personal aesthetic was on display as soon as I arrived to his headquarters in Manhattan's Flatiron neighborhood: instead of the usual hard angles and straight lines that are par for the course in corporate waiting rooms, his was furnished with a homey sofa, a coffee table with books about decor, potted plants, and a couple of large paintings that would not have looked out of place on the sales floor at Christie's. His own office, surrounded by big windows and anchored by comfortable seating areas, resembled a chic prewar studio apartment, save for the glass wall that exposed it to the rest of the floor.

"Typically our production time line is longer," van Wyck said, noticing that the gala was little more than a month away. Everyone was mindful of staying on track: this was a pro bono project, and nonprofits rely heavily on events for their yearly fundraising. "We are trying to help them make money, working as volunteers and essentially only covering our costs. So we have to focus on broad brushstrokes that have a big effect and can be achieved with a reasonable budget. The upside is that because of that, we don't have a long approval process, which saves time. They know we are going to do a good job."

Still, there were some kinks to iron out. A few key members of van Wyck's team walked in and sat around a rough-hewn table positioned in front of a bookcase teeming with art, history, and design books. There is no one path to becoming an event planner—while specializations in hospitality, production, or design can be helpful, no degree or special license is required—so it was interesting to see how everyone came from dramatically different backgrounds. Austin Ibasfalean, one of van Wyck's senior deputies who was overseeing the project, had worked at Ralph Lauren for almost eight years and then for the luxury titan LVMH in store design and visual merchandising. Anna Lund, van Wyck's director of partnerships, public relations, and special projects, had studied English literature—her graduation thesis, about the differences in English and American manners as seen through the works of Jane Austen and Edith Wharton, may have foreshadowed some of her future interests. Em Pak, who was in charge of props and construction, had gone to school for industrial design and specialized in large-scale installations.

Ibasfalean distributed detailed floor plans of the raw space they needed to transform. Architectural drawings, he explained, are critical to every project—the team uses them to brainstorm ideas and track ongoing changes in the design process. Everyone in the company takes computer-aided-design (CAD) classes so they can understand and update these plans and address everything from lighting choices to whether there is enough room for waiters to pass in between tables. "The difficulty in this case is that the space is an enormous old trading room with rubber floors and a forty-foot-tall acoustic tile ceiling with no rigging points," Ibasfalean said. "That means there is no way to lower the ceiling or hang lights from it. When you have a room that is so enormous, where you are trying to create an intimate atmosphere, it becomes very challenging."

Usually Van Wyck weighs in on the venues, but in this case Creative Time had selected 300 Vesey in advance. The vastness of the space did, however, afford some opportunities. "The plus side is we have the ability to create a progression as guests arrive and make their way to cocktails and dinner," Pak said. "We can really delineate different areas, each with its own aesthetic feel." Van Wyck got a quick rundown from Ibasfalean of where the project stood, suggested a few adjustments, and then called Justine Ludwig, Creative Time's director, on speakerphone to take her through the proposed design. She, too, had the floor plans in hand.

"Basically, what we are doing is taking Jenny Holzer as the starting point and bringing as much of her energy and vision to life without being reductive or overly referential," van Wyck said after pleasantries had been exchanged. "We are managing the very specific qualities of this space to make it function and to support important visual elements.

At the same time, we have to lay out areas that feel gracious and comfortable. People should feel the grandness of the space but also have pockets of intimacy and warmth, which it obviously lacks in its raw form." He paused for emphasis, then drilled down into specifics.

"The first thing we are doing is a palate cleanser, which is to say immediately transport guests somewhere special after their quite dry arrival to that corporate office building. So as soon as they get out of the elevator we will have a tunnel made of heavy black fabric, and we will use gates of lights changing color to create a progression. The idea is it's a staged visual journey out of your day and into a night of fun."

That tunnel led to an anteroom where cocktails and light hors-d'oeuvres would be served. Before the call, van Wyck had questioned the positioning of some potted plants that dotted the space. "Once people emerge from the tunnel there will be a center line of bar tables with stools," he said. "In the floor plans you can see that around the perimeter of the room there are some green trees—we now want to cluster those to create an allée going down the middle, with a pair of bars facing each other." Van Wyck explained that to solve the dilemma of how to light the space, dinner would be served in an adjacent room, under a canopy of trees lit from within; the foliage would feel both dramatic and cozy. Dining tables would be different shapes and sizes, some in snakelike configurations, others straight, and would be decorated with masses of candles. ("Candlelight makes everyone look young and beautiful. Your guests will be so grateful!") Because Holzer's work is so spare, it was understood that there would be no candelabra or tapered candles, but simple, unobtrusive votives in no-nonsense—and budget-friendly—glass receptacles.

The most complicated question was how to separate the cocktail area and dining room in a way that was practical yet impactful. "The division between cocktails and dinner is a wall of staggered mirrors, some eight feet tall, some twelve, some ten, some on one plane, others on a different plane," van Wyck said. "They will create endless reflections, playing with people's perceptions of the party and themselves." Anticipating concerns about over-served partygoers stumbling into the mirrors and creating a distracting bloodbath, van Wyck was quick to explain that the mirrors were actually made of Mylar, a synthetic material that is much lighter than glass and doesn't shatter. Still, the faux mirrors would need supports to stay upright, and concealing those was an issue.

"We are going to make a gigantic mound of fallen autumn leaves in different colors, positioned at the base of the mirrors and running the whole length of the room," van Wyck said. "When it's time we will pull open parts of the mirror wall and guests will walk through the leaves and into the dinner, leaving behind them a trail of foliage." After that, while everyone ate, the cocktail area would be restaged with a darker, cooler vibe, and glow-in-the-dark tape would delineate a dance floor for the after-party.

Once the presentation was done, all eyes turned from van Wyck to the speakerphone at the center of the table, as if it had a life of its own. "That sounds great," Ludwig said after a short pause. Everyone exhaled, and the shoulders in the room dropped an inch or two. "I love the tunnel— the transition out of the corporate building adds interest," she continued, before subtly hemming and hawing. "In the cocktail area the two big bars are great, but I don't quite understand the trees along the high-top tables. And I'm having a hard time visualizing the mounds of leaves, because Jenny's work is so clean and sleek."

Van Wyck elaborated on his train of thought. "We thought the leaves would be a great way to solve a functional problem, and at the same time they connect to the illuminated trees. Jenny sometimes presents her work outside, so there is a part of what she does that relates to nature. We are trying to put forward elements that are in line with her aesthetic but that also soften the venue. If this event were taking place in, say, an old Italian palazzo with decaying plaster, then we wouldn't need to worry about that." Pak pointed out that the leaves would make the room feel more ephemeral, referencing the passing of time. But, understandably for someone who doesn't deal with decorative deciduous foliage on a regular basis, Ludwig struggled with the concept. "I get that both Jenny's work and the space are quite stark, so we do need elements to warm things up," she said. "But I just can't visualize it." Van Wyck offered to email her some images that would give her a better idea of what he had in mind but also assured her that he would brainstorm other possibilities.

The rest of the discussion was perfunctory: table sizes and shapes, types of seating, number of guests per table. All seemed settled until Ludwig said that one of the bars was too big; she wasn't sure the budget would allow for that many bartenders. It didn't seem like much, but I sensed that van Wyck had flagged the comment. As good-byes were exchanged, he recommended, in a seemingly lighthearted way, that Ludwig not skimp on the bar staff. "I just have to say, if anyone has to wait in line for a drink, it will ruin all of the wonderful things we are doing," he said. There were chuckles all around, but it was clear he was only half joking.

A couple of weeks later, Lund and I drove to van Wyck's warehouse in New Jersey, about forty minutes outside of Manhattan. Most event planners rent their supplies; it's uncommon for them to stockpile or fabricate their own, so I was curious to see how that side of the operation worked. After crossing the Hudson River and skirting by the Newark airport, we turned onto a dreary industrial road and eventually pulled into a parking area large enough for trucks. The warehouse looked like, well, a warehouse, surrounded by other identical warehouses.

The inside, though, was a different story. It brought to mind Willy Wonka's factory, minus the chocolate river and candy mushrooms. Not that this was any less surreal: for starters, there were pterodactyls hanging out by the rafters above the entrance. "I have no idea what they were used for," Lund said, as she unsuccessfully attempted to suppress a giggle. She also couldn't quite figure out where she had last seen the Chinese gong resting against a wall, the taxidermy antelope that seemed to keep guard of a hallway, or the life-size gorilla made out of silver and gold pine needles.

She explained that the birdcages, butterflies, chandeliers, Mardi Gras beads, faux tortoiseshells, straw hats, corals, chinoiserie lanterns, baskets, seashells, rock crystals, life preservers, mirrors, and other knickknacks were in constant rotation, depending on special requests. (Nautical beach party! Circus-themed birthday! Destination wedding!) Lund had a feeling that a structure that I couldn't quite place but looked oddly familiar was part of an airport luggage carousel. "It might have been something for a party we did for an airline," she speculated.

What she did definitely recognize was the room that looked like a Greek archeological dig. "All this was for Bronson's forty-fourth birthday party," she said. By "all this" Lund meant a throne fit for Zeus, a Trojan horse, a gargantuan foot that might have been amputated from a colossus, and enough columns, plinths, pediments, and cornices to rebuild the Acropolis. In 2018, that and much more had been assembled on Mykonos, where van Wyck had decided that a disused smelting plant on a cliff by the sea was the perfect setting for a Homeric ball. The factory was in such poor shape that before any plans could even be considered, it had to be made structurally safe for human habitation, however temporarily; it also had no access roads, so van Wyck built one, using dynamite and a bulldozer. By the time he was done, the decrepit structure had been transformed into an Olympian setting complete with hand-painted frescoes. Hundreds of guests dressed as their favorite mythological figures were treated to performances by Duran Duran and Flo Rida and danced on island platforms in a flooded, laser-lit cave worthy of Hades until a breakfast of scrambled eggs, bagels, and osetra caviar was served. (Van Wyck was Dionysus, of course, in a grape-laden crown and turquoise toga with more grapes tumbling down the front.)

The warehouse, however, was no mere prop storage unit. Everywhere you turned there were people deeply engaged in one task or another. At one end of the ground floor, Marjeth Cummings oversaw the floral department, which had the air of a store within a store. It housed hundreds, if not thousands, of vases of all sizes, shapes, and finishes: mirrored, silver, gold, copper, plain, textured, clear, with and without handles.

"We have three events this week," Cummings said. "We get the flowers from the wholesaler, and then we arrange them the day before the event. Sometimes we make a test arrangement beforehand and send it to the client for approval." This initial sample, she explained, was usually based around a simple keyword, or even just a color or vase preference. In many other cases, though, the clients had already established a level of trust, and Cummings exercised her own judgment. "Many of us who have worked here a long time instinctively understand the van Wyck aesthetic, so we know in which general direction to go," she said. I asked what that meant exactly. "In terms of flowers it's about a loose elegance, with color, very natural, and not convoluted. We don't do anything that's heavily constructed or tight."

To Cummings's left, a colleague was taping amber cellophane onto clear glass containers; further afield, someone was covering a plain wood tabletop with marbleized paper, to surprisingly realist effect. "There are a lot of illusions being created here," Lund said. "I was a dancer growing up, and to me this looks like a stage set. I'd love to know how many hundreds of thousands of votive candles we have used over time, or how many tons of glitter. This year, just for the Save Venice ball, we covered huge Renaissance goddess statues with hundreds of pounds of red glitter!"

Upstairs there were even more workshops, including a full-blown sewing atelier surrounded by shelves packed with bolts of fabric in every color and animal pattern known to humanity. Having this in-house studio, Lund explained, gave van Wyck the ability to offer custom-made curtains, cushions, tablecloths, and upholstery, manufacture them quickly, then reuse or repurpose them as needed. The same applied to furniture. Not only did the warehouse have an extensive array of sofas, chairs, ottomans, benches, and beds ready to be shipped at a moment's notice, but also an entire carpentry shop. The sound of power-sawing and hammering was never far off.

A genial woman named Kim Ray gave us a tour. She

said her title was Production Stylist, but it might as well have been Astonishing Creations Overlord. The day we visited, she was working on, among other things, animal topiaries with a "Narnia vibe"; a Sleeping Beauty Christmas tree with a bed inside it, which was partially inspired by a Salvador Dalí glittered lobster tree she had previously done (it was finished off with an ocelot-print tree skirt); and a small herd of tartan deer resting on a bed of gold-leafed horns. Ray explained that she was especially fond of fabric animals: her father was a taxidermist, so she knew her way around plastic mounts that could be manipulated to create all sorts of creatures.

Just as in the New York office, where there were deputies who managed every aspect of a project, in the warehouse there were production leads making sure that all the necessary props and supplies were deployed. That, in a nutshell, was how Ray described her role. "And, I'm really good at putting furniture together," she added unnecessarily, as she showed me an assortment of sofas, banquettes, light fixtures, wine barrels, disco balls, and bars, as well as a thirty-foot dragon-embellished screen that came with a matching, similarly sized dragon.

The less creative part of the job was to make sure that

the inventory was properly returned and stored—if ever you needed, say, a chandelier made out of colored glass bottles at the last minute, it helped to know exactly where it was. There was also crew management to consider—how many drapers and carpenters would be required per project, and when? Did you need to stagger their work? How many bolts of vinyl? Was all the seating available in-house, or did anything need to be supplemented through an outside vendor? Production leads in the warehouse were constantly liaising with their Manhattan counterparts, and they too relied on the constantly evolving floor plans for guidance.

As Lund and I concluded our visit and Ray walked us out of the warehouse, I did a double take as I noticed part of a curvaceous vessel protruding from a small alleyway to the side of the building. "Oh, you hadn't seen the gondola?" Ray asked. I approached to discover that it was, indeed, an actual Venetian gondola, which looked surprisingly large and voluptuous outside of its natural watery habitat. "We're making a tarp to protect it from the elements. Bronson's parents got it for him for his birthday and had it shipped here." Just in case you're ever in need of a gift idea.

On our way back to Manhattan, I asked Lund what van Wyck paid the most attention to when tackling a project.

"There is always a big overarching idea to make people feel that they have traveled somewhere special for a night, but there are also elements that are much simpler but really important—for example, Bronson always says that lighting can instantly transform a room," Lund said, as images of my cavernous apartment flashed through my mind. "If you go into the Plaza Hotel ballroom with all the lights on, it can seem underwhelming, but it's a different thing when some are on, some off, and others dimmed so that they barely flicker. Lighting creates a sense of drama and it's a relatively inexpensive thing to do." Lund was echoing something that Pak had said in passing when I first met her: that the three key considerations for any event, regardless of budget or scale, were lighting, temperature control, and access to bars.

At the Creative Time Gala, I made a point of studying the lighting; it was so warm and uniform that you didn't notice it at all. Everyone, as van Wyck had promised, seemed to have a dewy glow. ("Great lighting should feel like there's no lighting.") The temperature, which allowed for both strapless dresses and long-sleeved velvet jackets, was also perfect, especially considering how decidedly imperfect the weather was outside; the trees in the main room seemed to sway almost imperceptibly, as they would in nature, though there weren't any visible fans. Then I compared the actual layout of the space to the floor plan I had seen weeks before. The basic idea was essentially the same, but the fall leaves were nowhere to be seen. Replacing them was a heavy black curtain that had been fabricated at the warehouse; it seemed to disappear within the space even as it divided it.

Toward the end of the evening I approached van Wyck, who was in high spirits and surrounded by friends. The party was a success: Creative Time had sold every table, Holzer had mentioned in her speech how beautiful the mise-en-scène was, and everyone was clearly having a good time. After congratulating him, I asked what had happened to the mound of leaves. His face went blank for a couple of seconds, as if he had absolutely no idea of what I was talking about. "Oh, the leaves!" he finally said, smiling. "You always have to have something in the plans for the clients to take out." He suggested we have another drink. As I approached the bar, I noticed that it was quite large, as originally planned, and more than adequately staffed. No one would have to wait in line.

I understood then why, during the entire call with Creative Time, I had detected a slight shift in van Wyck's tone only when Ludwig had considered a smaller bar: for all of the incredible scenarios and extravagant fantasies that van Wyck can concoct, comfort comes first. Leaves and mirrors are not essential for a great party; drinks and efficient service are. A few days later, the specific contours of the Creative Time Gala had receded in my mind, but a general sense of satisfaction remained. I wondered how van Wyck had learned to achieve this in such a seemingly natural way. It was as if he had absorbed the nuances of entertaining at a very early age, the way regular kids have to master their ABC's or multiplication tables. As it turns out, that wasn't far from the truth.

CHAPTER TWO

Van Wyck grew up with his parents, Mary Lynn and Bronson Sr., and his sister, Mimi, on a farm named Arrowhead outside of Tuckerman, a tiny town in Arkansas with fewer than two thousand inhabitants. Their closest neighbors were his grandparents, who lived three miles away.

Perhaps this isn't the origin story you were expecting for someone in van Wyck's urbane line of work. Rest assured, he was no ordinary farm boy. Van Wyck's family was one of the original and most prominent Dutch settlers in New York. If you've ever flown into or out of JFK Airport, you've driven on the Van Wyck Expressway. It is named after Robert Anderson van Wyck, who became the first mayor of New York City in 1898, after its five boroughs consolidated. In addition to the highway, there is a subway station and a middle school in Queens named after those early van Wycks.

Arrowhead wasn't a regular mom-and-pop homestead,

either. It was one of the largest farms in Arkansas, and the cotton, corn, rice, and soybeans it produced were sold all over the world. Some of van Wyck's uncles and cousins also lived on the property, which was made up of contiguous smaller farms, and relatives often visited from Little Rock. Van Wyck's paternal grandmother had moved down from New York and lived in an apartment in his maternal grandparents' house. She, too, often had friends staying with her.

"I just can't believe that kind of life existed," van Wyck says now. "You had every age group—grandparents, siblings, cousins, uncles . . ." It could have been chaos, but it wasn't, possibly thanks to one unbreakable family rule. "We all had to have one meal a day together, whether it was lunch or dinner—though we called lunch 'dinner' and dinner 'supper,'" van Wyck says. "It happened in different relatives' houses; there was a sort of rotation. On any given day, we might have had two dozen people at the table." Van Wyck's family had experience with hospitality even before then. In the early 1960s, the Army Corps of Engineers dammed a river in Arkansas, creating a large lake. Van Wyck's grandfather and great-grandfather developed a resort named Eden Isle on its shore with a hotel, the Red Apple Inn, as its centerpiece. The men ran the business side of it, while van

Wyck's great-grandmother oversaw guest relations and the staff at the award-winning restaurant.

During his childhood, van Wyck experienced a way of life that was equal parts eccentric, sophisticated, and homey. When his parents got married, in 1969, Bronson Sr., a ranked tennis player who would go on to graduate from Harvard Business School, wore his Marine Corps dress uniform, complete with the Bronze Star and the two Purple Hearts that he had been awarded during his service in Vietnam. Mary Lynn was in a Pauline Trigère dress with an eight-foot-long train, and her bridesmaids wore blue Pappagallo dresses with patchwork skirts. But all the guests had to carry candles, since there was no electricity in the dilapidated clapboard church that they had chosen for the ceremony. Years later, *Town & Country* called the wedding one of the best of the twentieth century.

The family lived in one of the most rural areas of the country; at the same time, van Wyck's grandfather owned Thoroughbred horses, and his grandmother ordered clothes from New York, Dallas, and Paris and tooled around in a black motorcycle with a sidecar. Van Wyck was surrounded by unusual pets, including goats, a potbellied pig, and a monkey. But he attended the local public school like any other kid and remembers that he and his sister were the only ones in their grade who had seen the ocean. "I was very lucky to have had that early education in Tuckerman, because the school was really small and the teachers cared so much. We got a lot of personalized attention," he says. "Plus, there was no way of becoming a jerk with other kids, as is often the case when you're that age in places like New York. You knew everybody and you knew you would see them all the time, so you had to be nice. We were also related to at least one hundred people in town."

There was a constant stream of friends from all over the world, including Arab racehorse breeders, Hong Kong businessmen, East Coast friends, foreign exchange students, artists, performers, and politicians, including longtime family friends Bill and Hillary Clinton. And if all those fascinating people were making the effort to come see you in the middle of Arkansas, where there was neither a hotel nor a restaurant in sight, you had better be able to properly entertain them at home.

"I remember we had a French student staying with us," van Wyck recalls. "So once a week we would have a meal in her honor, every time with food from a different part of France—Normandy, Brittany, Alsace, wherever. And one time we had a French Revolution dinner. We came dressed as *citoyens* and had to learn 'La Marseillaise.' We even had little tricorn hats. I thought it was very cute, but my grandmother from New York was horrified." Any occasion, in fact, was an excuse for theatrical reenactments and performances. There were props and costumes for Christmas (animals in a manger, Santa's elves); Thanksgiving (pilgrims and Native Americans); Easter (bunnies—live or make-believe); and Halloween (an old shed in the woods converted into a haunted house).

It wasn't all fun and games, though; everyone had to pitch in. One particular summer, van Wyck was given one of the most arduous tasks of all: separating the "red rice" from the white. "Red rice is actually brown," van Wyck says. "That's just what they call it. It's a genetic mutation that's rare—it probably happens in three or so plants out of a thousand. But the price for the crop was based on its purity, because the big companies did not want to sell a box of white rice with even a bit of brown in it." At the time, there wasn't a machine to separate the offending rice, so van Wyck had to do it by hand before the harvest. "The best thing was to pull out the rice plant and get the whole head, which has a couple hundred pieces of rice on it. So you would wade into the fields, which were flooded, you had hip boots on and were carrying a shovel or a hoe, you'd find the red rice and get rid of that plant. It was backbreaking work, you were in water at least up to your shins, and there were snakes everywhere."

It was always understood that when van Wyck turned thirteen he would go away for school. "My parents had gone to boarding school themselves, and they never even presented not going as an option," he says. He enrolled at Groton School in Massachusetts, and after that he headed to Yale, where he majored in history. More than academics, though, van Wyck's main interest seemed to be shaking up the collegiate social scene.

I'm not talking about your average keg parties. Always eager to team with a theme, van Wyck once covered his entire apartment in tin foil, à la Warhol's Factory, for a party to celebrate the thirtieth anniversary of the day Edie Sedgwick met Andy Warhol. For a Narnia winter wonderland, he dragged in a pool liner and covered it with crushed ice and snow—a concept that proved less than successful as the evening wore on and the decor melted into a slushy mess.

Back then van Wyck had no sense that he would make a profession out of his talent for having a good time. But in retrospect, many of his choices, which might have initially felt haphazard, seem like pieces of a puzzle coming together. Although he was by no means a focused student—likely because of the gusto with which he pursued his extracurricular activities—van Wyck did love his major, and history plays a big role in what he does now. His productions are often informed by his knowledge of Belle Époque France, ancient Greece, Ptolemaic Egypt, or Pre-Columbian America. His first stint out of college, an internship in the State Department, also ended up being more valuable than he could have known at the time. In the early nineties, van Wyck landed in

Paris under the auspices of Pamela Harriman, who was then the American ambassador to France. She also happened to be one of the most fascinating, talked-about women in politics and society during the twentieth century.

Harriman, whose given surname was Digby, married Winston Churchill's son, Randolph, in 1939. During the war, while her husband was on deployment in North Africa, she sheltered at 10 Downing Street with the prime minister and his wife, Clementine, and began an affair with Franklin Roosevelt's special envoy to Great Britain, Averell Harriman. Her relationship with Randolph ended shortly thereafter, and Pamela embarked on a long string of well-publicized affairs with some of the most powerful men of the era, becoming a powerful social figure in her own right. In 1971, recently widowed from a marriage to a Broadway producer, she married Averell, her original paramour. During the 1970s and '80s, the Harrimans became big supporters of the Democratic Party, hosting receptions, dinners, and fundraisers in their Georgetown home. Averell died in 1986, but Pamela continued with her political involvement, and in 1993 Bill Clinton made her ambassador to France. She died in Paris, of a brain hemorrhage, in 1997.

Van Wyck had the unique opportunity to work with Harriman as she coordinated receptions at the embassy. Through her he was able to understand that being a successful host has as much to do with diligence as with natural ability. Harriman kept a file with thousands of index cards full of information about all the important people she had met. The cards were constantly updated so that every day, during her many ambassadorial interactions, she could strike a seemingly natural conversation with whomever she encountered, "remembering" that person's hobbies, children's names, and other personal and professional details.

Official functions required this kind of personalized care, considering that Harriman received guests as varied as Bill Gates, Catherine Deneuve, Valentino, Prince Rainier of Monaco, and the Comte de Paris, who was the pretender to the French throne. Van Wyck assisted in the daily ritual of updating the cards and with the delicate business of devising dinner seating charts, learning about protocol and honing that special talent that lets you know why it is inconceivable that so-and-so should sit next to so-and-so, or absolutely essential that they do.

The last of van Wyck's postcollegiate adventures was in Los Angeles, where he landed hoping to become an actor, but eventually settled into a studio gig. "My title was Creative Executive, which is funny because you were neither creative nor an executive," he says. "My job was to read scripts and attach talent to them." Even then, van Wyck's attention lay elsewhere. At the time, no invitation was more coveted than to the *Vanity Fair* party immediately after the Academy Awards ceremony. Van Wyck managed to crash the bash every year he lived in LA. On one occasion he rented an Oscar statuette and had a nameplate made for it that said "Bronson van Wyck/Sound Editing." He then hired a limo, called a group of friends to serve as his entourage, and simply ambled into the party, Oscar held high.

Just as when he was at Yale, word got out that van Wyck loved to party. At work, his favorite task was helping to organize premieres and studio events. But the idea that he could do that for a living hadn't clicked. "It was a very new profession at the time," he says. "I was just starting to hear about people like Robert Isabell, who were called event planners, and that this was becoming an industry. I knew about famous people who had thrown legendary parties back in the day, but they had done it themselves, because they had had huge staffs of their own. But in the modern era no one has footmen and butlers and underbutlers, so that kind of service had to be outsourced. That was really taking off at the time. Now I joke to friends and clients that I am their temporary butler."

Van Wyck's career path came into focus after a conversation with his mother. It was a Sunday night, and he was feeling miserable, having neglected ten scripts he was supposed to have read for a morning meeting the following day. "There was no way I was going to get through them, so I was on the phone complaining to my mother," he says. Mary Lynn was at home in Arkansas, having recently recovered from a tough bout with cancer. "She had to focus exclusively on getting better for two years, so I think she was ready to be out in the world again," van Wyck says. "She asked me, well, what would you have done this weekend if you could have done anything you wanted?" Van Wyck didn't have to think about it. "I would have thrown a party," he said. Mary Lynn's response was equally swift. "Well, then let's figure out a way to throw parties and get paid for it."

CHAPTER THREE

Van Wyck got his big break a few months after that fateful conversation with his mother. His good friend Marina Rust, a writer and contributing editor at *Vogue*, was getting married in Dark Harbor, Maine, and preparations were not going smoothly—no one seemed to understand her desire for unpretentious yet elegant simplicity. "She was having trouble with all the arrangements, so I gave her some advice, told her what I thought she did and didn't need," van Wyck recalls. "Then she called me the next day and said, 'I've let everyone go and I want you to do it.'"

Van Wyck was on the other side of the country and the wedding was less than a month away, but he immediately gave notice at the studio. While he headed out to execute a plan, Mary Lynn loaded up a U-Haul with rugs, vases, tables, and all sorts of other furnishings, accessories, and decorations that they had stored in an old barn on their farm, and she drove it from Arkansas to Maine. Logistics were especially

complicated because Dark Harbor is located on the tiny island of Islesboro—population five hundred—and local event
infrastructure was nonexistent. Van Wyck arranged for a
band to come up on a whaler boat, hired a chef to fly over
and cook, and convinced the local school to let him use their
yellow buses to ferry around the three hundred or so guests.
The frenzied preparations went on until minutes before the
ceremony, but ultimately the weekend was a big success. The
wedding was even featured over several pages in *Vogue*.

Van Wyck's agreement with Mary Lynn was that she
would fly to Arkansas after the wedding and he would drive
the U-Haul back. On the way down from Maine, he decided
to stop and stay for a few days with his sister, Mimi, who
had also pitched in at the wedding but at the time was an in-
tern in the Clinton White House. Because of the Clintons'
Arkansas roots, van Wyck and Mimi had known Bill and
Hillary their whole lives—in fact, in 1992, as a summer job,
van Wyck had been Hillary's photographer and handled her
correspondence. When the Clintons heard that van Wyck
was in town, they invited him and his sister for drinks.
"They wanted to check up on my mother's health, and see
what we were up to," van Wyck says. He mentioned his new
career plans, and the Clintons immediately suggested he

stick around. "They said, 'Well, you know, we throw a lot of parties around here!'"

As it turns out, van Wyck ended up working more for Al and Tipper Gore than for the Clintons. It was the end of 1999, and the Gores were gearing up for the presidential election the following year. Van Wyck camped out at Mimi's place in Washington and started helping however he could. "The first event I did for the Gore campaign was in February, and then I worked with them all that spring," he says. Serendipitously, the Democratic National Convention was taking place in Los Angeles, where van Wyck still had his apartment. He was hired as the director of events for the convention and given responsibility for all the Democratic National Committee events. Once the convention started, van Wyck oversaw sixteen functions in five days.

That fall, hopeful that his candidate would go on to win the national election, van Wyck moved again to Mimi's couch in Georgetown and started planning Gore's presidential inauguration. Of course, things didn't turn out quite as he—and millions of others—had hoped. But there was a silver lining. "There are only about eleven weeks between the election and the inauguration," van Wyck says. "But in this case, there was a gap of four weeks when no one knew who the president would be. Then the Supreme Court made its decision, and it was announced that George Bush would be president." Out of the blue, van Wyck received a call from the Bush team asking if he could help.

"At that point we were just twenty days out," van Wyck says. The entire thing, which included four days of events, was budgeted at about $60 million. Out of that, Congress allocated $15 million to cover the actual inauguration ceremony; the rest had to come from private donors. Bush's inaugural committee had lists of business leaders and friends who wanted to support the occasion, and van Wyck helped create a series of tiered schedules for their participation. "If you were a donor at x level, you got to attend, for example, a lunch," he says. "But if you gave more than x, you got to do that plus something else, or go to a more intimate dinner instead. Essentially, we worked with the inaugural committee to create sponsorship packages that could be sold. And then we were in charge of producing the events that made up those packages."

Van Wyck not only managed to put everything together in time but also came in $3 million under budget. "The money that is not spent goes to charity, so of course everyone was very happy about that." So happy, in fact, that he received an honor he could not have expected: a Presidential

Inaugural Medal. Not bad for someone with a wedding and a couple of movie premieres under his belt.

Shortly after that, van Wyck moved to New York and experimented with different aspects of the event planning business. "Initially, we sometimes agreed to do catering, or hire chefs and waiters for an event that was already in progress," he says. "But very quickly we realized that everyone thinks they're experts when it comes to food. Everybody eats three meals a day and everyone has an opinion, so no matter how good your miso cod is, someone is not going to like cod. You're never going to please everyone. Also, with catering, the point of contact between you and your clients and their guests is the waitstaff, and temporary cater-waiters are usually doing that job while they pursue whatever their true dream is. I don't hold that against them, but I don't want to depend on people who are just there for one night. They reflect on you, but you have very little control over how they perform."

Van Wyck decided to focus instead on event design, which aligned more with his personal passions. Planners would hire him to take care of the space for their parties—but even that, van Wyck quickly realized, came with its own set of problems. "With design, we were providing a product, a real, tangible thing, but in the high-stress, emotionally charged process of producing an event, the party planner, who was providing a valuable service but in some ways an intangible one, would sometimes have a fear that his role wasn't sufficiently visible," van Wyck says. "So there would be an inevitable moment when he had to prove his value to the client by somehow creating a crisis out of something that wasn't a crisis so that he could be seen solving it. Also, anybody in the world can hang up a sign and say they're a party planner, and as long as they have clients they can work. It's great that it's an accessible industry, but that also means that not everyone is as competent or professional as they should be."

One experience in particular broke the camel's back. "My mother and I were working on a party in 2003 at the New York Public Library," van Wyck says. "It was the middle of winter and there was a big blizzard. Everyone knows that there's only one loading dock at the library—it's through a tiny gate that originally was meant for carriages, and it's so narrow that you actually have to take the mirrors off your truck to get in." As instructed, van Wyck and Mary Lynn arrived at six in the morning to unload all the decor—except that there were about five or six other trucks simultaneously pulling in. "It was lighting, catering, rentals, sound, ice, everyone else plus us, all at the same time!" van Wyck says, still annoyed at the thought. "The party planner hadn't done a schedule for arrivals at this one very limited space."

To top things off, it turned out that on that very same day the library was moving out forty thousand books through that same loading dock. "Of course their needs were paramount, because it was their space. Nothing had been coordinated at all. There were six hundred or eight hundred people coming that evening, and Mom and I were just sitting there, doing nothing in a freezing truck for hours." Finally, van Wyck had no choice but to hand-carry everything himself directly from the street. "I said to my mother, we are never going to be in this situation again. That's when we decided we needed to oversee ourselves every part of the events we worked on."

The guiding principle he set for himself was simple, and it's as relevant now as it was then: Just do whatever it takes to get everything right. Van Wyck often describes his company's work ethos by saying, "Once we feel like we've done enough, we do more." That's why, he says, his company is structured in a different way than most in the field. "There is a business model where you just pull together teams as needed, for each event, and rent whatever furniture you need, so you have very little overhead," he says. "That's not us. We work with a bespoke, luxury, service-driven model, so we need to have full-time employees and our own assets. We find ourselves a lot of times taking care of things that we don't particularly want to do, and some that aren't even profitable from a business perspective. But we do it all because we just want to work in a certain way, and that's what sets us apart." That's why the warehouse I visited in New Jersey is so important. It enables van Wyck to maintain a consistent level of quality, from the flowers to the banquettes to the lights and props and even the tablecloths and cutlery.

Having his own inventory is also essential when he organizes events abroad—something not many in the industry are able to do. Event planning is ultimately a local business, which is why every town has a go-to wedding specialist that does a sort-of-okay job in the same old boring venues, serving the same old rubber chicken. Only a handful of event planners have the kind of connections, built over time and through experience, that allow them to source high-quality props, building materials, caterers, and temporary employees all over the world.

"When we have a wedding in England or France we ship little to nothing because there are wonderful things that we can use in those countries," van Wyck says. "If we are going to Mexico there are great resources for technical equipment and props of a certain vernacular style; but it would be very hard to do, say, a Viennese Bauhaus party in Mexico using local supplies, so in that case we would ship some of our own stuff. And then there are places like Saint Barth's, where we bring absolutely everything, down to the napkins."

Another point of difference is the amount of people he assigns to each project. "The fact that we have a substantial, full-time staff probably makes us less profitable, because we put about a person and a half in every position, but that's essential for us," van Wyck says. "We purposely overstaff and oversupport." Although he works in creative and personal services, where attitudes can be somewhat informal, van Wyck says his company communicates with clients like a white-shoe law firm in terms of details and consistency, recapping every meeting with minutes and writing memoranda. "It's a luxury to engage a company like ours, and that means that the process of working with us needs to be an integral part of the experience," Van Wyck says. "The party is what you think of as the product we sell, but I believe that the interactions leading up to it have to feel as luxurious as the event itself."

To start the planning process, the most important thing the client needs to do is firmly establish the amount of guests. "It's not the same thing to take fifty people on a psychedelic journey inspired by seventies pre-disco flower power as it is to take two hundred people to the same place," van Wyck says. "I would do everything very differently in those two situations." The next steps are creating a planning calendar, doing a venue analysis, and estimating the budget. "Until the space is agreed upon it's hard to design a flow and aesthetic, so the selection of the venue has to happen very early on," he says. "If we know we are doing a tent then we have a blank slate and we can get a jump start on design even if we don't know where it will be located." Another thing that can't be left to the last minute is entertainment. "There is only one Lady Gaga, one Alabama Shakes, and one Jimmy Vali Orchestra, so if your heart's set on someone specific, you want to book that early so you don't end up having to plan everything around that performer's availability."

As he addresses those practical considerations, van Wyck also conducts a quasi-forensic investigation of his clients' tastes and wants, inquiring about their favorite films, hotels, historical periods, furniture styles, and destinations. "Using that information, we start focusing on the overarching creative direction of the party," van Wyck says. "That narrative ends up answering all other questions along the way—the menu, decorations, dress code, and invitations flow out of it." The end goal is that each and every event should feel completely personalized. "Of course I know what I like, but I'm not throwing a party for myself," van Wyck says.

If need be, van Wyck and his team can whip up an event in three weeks, but the usual time frame is more like three to six months. "The more time we have, the more personal the party becomes, because we can draw out details that are reflective of the host's personality," van Wyck says. "And obviously, if it's a destination event and people have to travel, you need extra time to give everyone a heads-up. That's a positive thing because it builds anticipation. And it's a gift to your guests when you can give them something to look forward to."

It's the clients who decide how and when they want to communicate. "Some prefer to text message me directly, others handle details through their assistants or chiefs of staff, others prefer only face-to-face," van Wyck says. "There are some projects where we see the client once, talk to them twice, and then we make the choices. When we have very little time we can be very efficient on how we engage the client and get them to share what they need." Other occasions require a great deal more hand-holding. Van Wyck remembers how, in preparation for one wedding, the mother of the bride requested to have a telephone call at 9:45 every single morning for eleven months. Some may have found this unnecessary, but not van

Wyck. "This was a really important moment in their family's life, and we were there to treat it as such," he says firmly.

Van Wyck understands the importance of family—many of the principles passed on to him by his parents and grandparents are at the core of how he interacts with clients. There is a substantial amount of social finesse and know-how that he passively acquired simply by growing up the way he did, and it would be disingenuous to suggest that certain family connections weren't instrumental in helping him land some of his first jobs. But it's worth noting that many of van Wyck's most successful peers didn't have privileged upbringings by any stretch of the imagination. As van Wyck mentioned, event planning is a labor-intensive industry with virtually no barriers to entry. Family influence can take you only so far if you're not talented and fully dedicated to the job.

Though the pros heavily outweigh the cons, van Wyck admits that there was a learning curve in running a family business. "You can't fire your mother or sister, so you have to make sure you get along," he says, laughing. "But the most important thing is that my mom, sister, and I really had to learn how to step back as we grew. A company with three family members and three employees is very different than one with three family members and thirty employees. In order for nonfamily members to feel invested and give one hundred percent, you have to remove the family dynamic from work. Everyone needs to be on equal footing in terms of advancement."

That entailed creating clearly defined roles, and sticking to them. Mimi was the company's chief operating officer—"the drill sergeant who kept the trains running on time," as van Wyck puts it—until she moved to Charleston about a decade ago. She opened an office there and currently oversees projects for clients who are not based in New York and whose events are not taking place in New York. ("If someone in Dallas wants to throw a party in Mexico, it doesn't matter at all that they are communicating with someone who is not in our New York office," van Wyck reasons.) Mary Lynn works mostly on design, coming up with creative ideas and collaborating on an array of projects with different managers. "She's also great with sourcing," van Wyck says. "She goes to antique markets, fairs, and garden shows, and finds amazing stuff." As for his own job description, van Wyck estimates that he spends three or four hours a day fielding creative and logistical questions. He also steps in to solve crises, leads initial contacts with most new clients, maintains relationships with long-standing ones, supervises overall quality control, and is responsible for "setting the standard, vision, and values of the company."

The best part of working with family, van Wyck says, is seeing someone you love do something they love. "It's as if you had a sister who was an opera singer and you got to see her perform at La Scala," he says. "I get to do that dozens of times a year, when I go to an event that my mom or my sister have put together, and I'm able to witness their skill and judgment and expertise."

Mimi and Mary Lynn might say the same about him. Even when he's not working, van Wyck is always welcoming people at home. His New York apartment is chockablock with glasses, china, candlesticks, and all manner of antiques and curiosities that often make it into his events but that also allow him to host large groups at the drop of a party hat. He even has a shell case from World War I that was repurposed as a giant cocktail shaker in order to make eight drinks at a time rather than the standard two. "Otherwise you're stuck behind the bar all night and can't talk to people," he says.

At the end of the day, entertaining is just part of van Wyck's DNA—a natural instinct. I was able to witness this firsthand at a tribute to the most meaningful clients he could ever possibly have: his own parents.

CHAPTER FOUR

———

We've all had to deal with a surprise party at one time or another. You know the drill: arrive early, hide, be quiet, yell all at once, don't be the annoying spoiler who shows up late and runs into the birthday boy in the elevator. If you're the one being surprised, pretend you didn't hear about it weeks ago, swear that you didn't have a clue it was happening when you ran into so-and-so holding a present in the elevator, and convince everyone that you're wearing that nice outfit by coincidence. If you're the one hosting, get some balloons, snacks, and a few bottles of champagne. Right?

Not quite, if you're a member of the van Wyck family. When Bronson and Mimi realized that their parents' fiftieth wedding anniversary was on the horizon, they started plotting a secret party for a few hundred friends in Palm Beach, Florida—a year in advance. The rigor with which the preparations were mapped out rivaled that of an army special ops mission. Because Mary Lynn is often in the New

York offices to collaborate on projects, a special code name was given to the event. Woe to anyone who slipped up.

I visited the van Wyck offices a few days before the weekend of the festivities to find out how things were coming along. Two young staffers, Mallory Young and Alix DeGraff, were headed to Florida the following day to set up. "There are two semis leaving tonight from our warehouse to Palm Beach," Young said matter-of-factly. She and De-Graff were the project managers, and they agreed to take me through the specifics. They also wound up giving me firsthand insight into what it takes to break into the event planning business, and discussed how to hold your own once you're in.

Appropriately enough, Young figured out she wanted to be an event planner—and specifically that she wanted to work for van Wyck—at a party. "It was a French-themed debutante ball in New Orleans, where I'm from, and they had Maroon 5 and Wiz Khalifa perform, which was amazing," Young said. But that wasn't what made her curious about the profession. Nor was it that guests arrived in a formal procession down the streets of New Orleans, accompanied by musicians, courtesans, and huntsmen on horseback. It wasn't even the Gallery of Stags that had been created at the venue, hung with more than fifty pieces of taxidermy, nor the trompe l'oeil façade of the ancient royal hunting lodge that stood where Louis XIV erected his famous Palace of Versailles, which masked an enormous tent behind it. And forget about the Hall of Mirrors, with its fifteen cut-crystal chandeliers hung over a silk-lined ballroom, complete with parquet flooring. No. What did it for Young was a visit to the bathroom.

"There was a tray with Band-Aids, hair ties, mints, bobby pins, individual Advil packets . . . everything a drunk girl could possibly need!" she recalled, smiling. "And I thought, whoever did this is amazing—it was as if they had thought of absolutely everything." Later on, she asked her friend to connect her with the evening's event planner—someone named Bronson van Wyck. Young was finishing school in Virginia and was prepared to move wherever she could land a job she loved. She sent a letter to van Wyck explaining how she had heard about him and why she wanted to work at his company. Here comes the good part, though. At the debutante ball, even in her state of, let's say, euphoria, Young had had the presence of mind to take a picture of that amenities tray in the bathroom; months later, she included it in her job application as proof that she knew and admired van Wyck's work. Soon after, van Wyck hired her as his assistant.

(Van Wyck's tips to get your foot in the door: "Spell-check your résumé; do more than what's expected; arrive early and stay late; be articulate; make eye contact; be grateful and show it." He's a big believer in internships, and points out that many Van Wyck & Van Wyck full-time employees started out as interns. "By the very nature of the industry, there is constantly a lot of movement.")

DeGraff arrived at the company in 2016, the same year as Young, after graduating from art school at the University of Michigan and interning at event planning companies in Chicago. At that time, van Wyck had just started his sister company, Workshop, which focused exclusively on corporate events, under the Van Wyck & Van Wyck umbrella. She started out as an assistant at Workshop but quickly realized that she strongly preferred private events. "We are all in the same office, and we are one team, but there is a different way of communicating with brands than with individuals," she explained. "Corporate has many guidelines and procedures that you have to follow, and when you form a relationship with the client it's more about learning about a company and working within their structure. It's very cut-and-dry: here is the budget, these are the deliverables. And usually they come with an idea already in mind and you just have to execute it and make it as good as possible."

With private events the rapport is different. "A big wedding can take a year or more to plan, so you get to know the client really well," DeGraff continued. "There is a certain chemistry that happens, and you quickly start to throw in suggestions. You have a lot more input and creativity. If someone is celebrating something big in their life and hiring Bronson, it's because they know the party will be out of this world. They want something that they couldn't have thought of themselves."

I pointed out that a normal day in the office for her and Young might literally be the most important moment in one of their clients' lives—and that everyone has a work snafu once in a while. Surely the prospect of dealing with that level of stress would weed out a great deal of people in their industry? Young and DeGraff glanced at each other conspiratorially. "It's definitely not a nine-to-five job," Young said. "Sometimes I can't sleep—definitely not the night before a big event. Or if I do sleep, I'll have nightmares." De-Graff seconded that. "I wake up in the middle of the night to use the notes section of my phone, suddenly realizing I forgot to add such-and-such an item to my rental order, or I didn't get any linens." She shrugged. "But overall I fall right back asleep."

Both Young and DeGraff mentioned a quality that is a natural prerequisite for their jobs: being a people pleaser. "You very often form meaningful, long-term, emotional attachments to your clients," DeGraff said. "You want to make them happy, and it's incredibly rewarding when they tell you what that special day meant to them." Another obvious requirement: strong organizational skills. "I've just always been a planner," Young said. "Even when I was a kid, I would arrange everything. If I was having a sleepover, I would make lists to see who to invite and what we would do. It's in my nature." She also pointed out that, with time, you learn how to identify real crises from temporary problems. In all likelihood, those linens that interrupted DeGraff's sleep weren't make-or-break. "You realize that clients think that every single decision is really, really important," Young said. "But, after a while, you know that's not the case. A live band is important; sushi isn't."

What's truly essential, however, is having the ability to improvise. It's a given that at some point—usually at the worst possible point—something will go wrong, and you will have to respond on the fly. DeGraff brought up a fiftieth birthday party for a client in New York. It was a big deal: a long cocktail hour, dinner, dancing, and a late-night performance by Run-DMC. Invitations had already gone out when, days before the event, the venue that the team had selected lost its liquor license. What to do? It was too late to start over. Van Wyck haggled and haggled, until he finally managed to obtain a temporary permit to serve alcohol, but only for two hours at the beginning of the evening. He found a second venue nearby to use after that permit expired, but that didn't solve the problem of how to explain a mid-evening migration to two hundred guests. Then came his stroke of genius. He moved Run-DMC's set to the beginning of the night and hired actors to impersonate police officers breaking up the gathering right after the performance ended. The alleged reason: a lack of a liquor license.

It worked. The guests, none the wiser about the backstory, were hauled into prison buses, which DeGraff had found and rented in New Jersey and Ohio. ("Try finding a prison bus complete with bars on the windows in New York City!") By then the faux police officers had relaxed, producing boom boxes and flasks for the ride. The buses arrived at the new venue, where the evening unfolded as originally planned. "What started as a problem ended up being an extra great element," DeGraff said. "Everyone thought it was a really fun idea and they never knew what we had gone through."

Hang out with event planners long enough and you'll hear plenty of stories like that. "Flyover planes give me such anxiety now," said Young, as if that were a common affliction. Turns out they are a really fun touch at outdoor weddings, if you can get them to swoop by with a Mr. and Mrs. So-and-So banner just as the newlyweds have finished reciting their vows. Not so fun if, say, a fog bank moves in from the sea, the pilot suddenly stops answering your calls, and you have to explain to the mother of the bride hours before the ceremony that there will be no plane, except that, wait . . . OMG, so much fun again when the plane miraculously appears after all, even though no one had called you back, and it all happens right after the kiss! ("Afterward I finally was able to get in touch with the plane rental company and said, 'Thanks, I guess?'" Young recalled.)

Van Wyck himself once had to stream AC/DC's "Highway to Hell" full blast into an uncooperative band's dressing room so they would come out and do their set as planned. When it occurred to Sean "Puffy" Combs, as his guests were about to arrive for his fortieth birthday celebration, that it would be cool to have snow falling indoors, van Wyck tracked down a snow machine in forty-five minutes and made it happen. Though you wouldn't know it by watching him at work, obsessing over every detail, van Wyck swears he has learned to relax somewhat—realizing, for example, that he can't control the weather. It's a good idea, he says, "to remember that your guests won't know what didn't happen."

It's also easier said than done. Despite all the precautions, his parents' fiftieth anniversary party nearly collapsed before it began. Van Wyck and Mimi had decided that they would try to invite everyone who had attended Bronson Sr. and Mary Lynn's wedding in 1969—never mind that they hadn't even met a few of those old family acquaintances—in addition to more recent friends. When they finally compiled the list, they sent out emails carefully specifying the surprise component, and that RSVPs should go only to van Wyck. It proved unfortunate, however, that van Wyck and his father share the same name: one guest mistakenly sent his response to Bronson Sr.'s email address. Thankfully, Mimi was in cc, and the siblings instantly sprang into action. Van Wyck called Dad and told him their office server had been infected with a devastating virus, and that under no circumstances should he open his emails. The company's IT expert then hacked into Bronson Sr.'s account and deleted the errant RSVP before he could read it.

Months later there were no such glitches. The commemorative weekend kicked off with a welcome dinner at the home of close friends of the van Wycks in Palm Beach. Everyone, save the couple of honor, was told to wear white, and Mary Lynn and Bronson Sr. were indeed taken aback to find hundreds of angelic figures waiting for them. The following evening was the pièce de résistance: a Zodiac-themed ball organized at the decorator Mimi McMakin's house on the shore of Lake Worth. Cocktails were served on the lawn overlooking the water, where enormous trees had been illuminated and festooned with tinsel that glittered like faraway galaxies. Lanterns were hung down from branches to form assorted patterns, blue beams created an otherworldly effect, and astrological motifs were projected onto the house itself.

Attendees had been asked to wear outfits inspired by their star signs—as he often does, van Wyck had created a website with a mood board for those in need of costume suggestions. Even in this crowd, which did not skew particularly young, everyone had taken the dictum seriously: there were leonine scarves, horned headpieces, bows and arrows, and matador capes everywhere you turned. (Since his parents weren't aware of the theme, van Wyck had flown down outfits for them—a red shirt, leather chaps, harness,

and impressive antlers for his Taurus father, and a more de-
mure aquatic-themed white blouse and sea-blue skirt with a
metallic fishing net overlay for his Pisces mother.) The waitstaff—men who clearly knew the inside of a gym—sported
skimpy togas and bare torsos. "Only Bronson would have
half-naked bartenders for his parents' fiftieth anniversary,"
one guest quipped, laughing. "But the thing is, his parents
love it, too!"

Van Wyck has a "twenty-minute rule" when it comes
to entertaining. He believes that, especially in today's era
of brief attention spans, things have to constantly move
along; even subtle changes in music or lighting can create
a new mood. To be sure, there was no shortage of stim-
uli that evening. Just as cocktail hour was winding down,
food stations were set up, offering everything from fried
chicken and macaroni and cheese to custom-made Caesar
salads. Dinner was a casual affair, with people holding small
plates in groups or relaxing on chaises on the grass. Shortly
afterward, Young, DeGraff, and the rest of van Wyck's crew,
recognizable by their light-up sneakers, gently ushered the
crowd into the party area.

By party area I mean the property's private chapel,
which that night exuded a decidedly nondenominational

vibe. A gigantic disco ball dominated the nave; what might have been the altar was now a stage, bedecked with a wall of pink flowers that contrasted with the violet and neon illumination; to the sides were vignettes featuring everything from giant paper butterflies to colorful parasols to large stuffed animals. Above the entrance hung a giant banner with the silhouette of a couple against a stained glass domed window forming a cross; the words "For Me and My Gal" were written underneath. Then the Elvis impersonator appeared.

Trust me, it all made sense, in an anything-goes sort of way. You were now on van Wyck's ride, and there was no point in getting off—nor would you have wanted to. Elvis did a rendition of "A Little Less Conversation" and then invited van Wyck's parents to join him onstage, where he informed them that they were renewing their vows, to a chorus of cheers. Needless to say, this wasn't a tear-jerking recommitment. Bronson Sr.: "I promise to always be your hunka-hunka-hunk-o-burning love." Mary Lynn: "I promise to always love you tender, and never treat you like a hound dog, unless you want me to." Light-up plastic rings were exchanged, and the couple gamely led the first dance to "All Shook Up."

Shortly after that it was van Wyck's turn to take to the microphone, in order to thank everyone who had made the trip to Palm Beach and to introduce the special performers of the evening: Ruth Pointer of the Pointer Sisters, her daughter Issa, and her granddaughter Sadako. The trio powered through classics like "I'm So Excited," "Automatic," and "Jump (For My Love)" as everyone sang along. When the indoor pyrotechnical displays indicated that the ladies had finished their set, deejays took over and van Wyck's twenty-minute rule really came into effect. Light-up sunglasses were distributed on the dance floor, then pastel-hued wigs, then tequila shots. Soon after that, an impressive array of desserts materialized: pecan pies, blueberry pies, profiteroles. It was as if a much-needed sugar rush had been perfectly timed to ensure everyone got a second wind—which was definitely the case.

The following day, I awoke just after the crack of noon. Feeling inexplicably unrefreshed, it occurred to me that the perfect thing to do in my fragile state would be to jump into the ocean. I hobbled out of bed and noticed a tote on the floor; it was the gift bag I'd been given as I left the party, which I had been too distracted to examine. Inside was a bathing suit, custom printed with the same tableau of the cosmos that had been on the invitation and projected onto the walls of the house during the party. The tag said, simply, "Van Wyck Zodiac Ball 2019." As I put on the trunks and headed to the beach, I couldn't help but think of what Young had said to herself when she was in the bathroom at her friend's party in New Orleans: it really was as if someone had thought of absolutely everything.

CHAPTER FIVE

nticipating people's needs and responding to them to the best of your ability is, ultimately, the essence of hospitality. Van Wyck likes to point out that this idea is referenced in practically every religion—failing to provide shelter is a big no-no. Remember how Jesus had to be born in a manger, surrounded by barn animals, because the local inn was supposedly fully booked? In the Book of Genesis, Sodom is destroyed after its wicked inhabitants harass two angels disguised as weary travelers rather than give them food and board. A similar story plays out in Greek mythology and Sanskrit epics: tattered wanderers turn out to be gods; great fortune is given to those who take them in, and destruction rains upon those who don't.

We could go even further back and argue that the ability to welcome others into our midst is part of what makes us human. Maybe a defining moment in the history of evolution took place when a couple of our earliest ancestors decided to gussy up a cave, throw a leg of something or other on the fire, and invite a few intimates for an at-home. Who knows? This book is not *Becoming an Anthropologist*. We can be certain, however, that successfully bringing together different people has been key in the development of every culture, across continents, for millennia.

How, then, do we track historical shindigs in a way that is useful to party planners today? And what eras should we focus on? The Roman Empire, with its no-holds-barred bacchanals, is tempting—but animal sacrifices, gladiatorial combat, and days-long orgies are no longer part of polite society. The Renaissance is generally regarded as the period in which modern manners were born, as a way of both enforcing order in burgeoning cities and distinguishing the privileged classes from the riffraff. Still, not all sixteenth- and seventeenth-century codes of conduct, such as using only three fingers rather than both hands to eat at the table, have withstood the test of time; and, for the most part, present-day hostesses have devised subtler ways of dealing with social rivals than poison rings. The court of Versailles, with its limitless budgets and endless carrying on, would have been a professional party giver's dream come true—but we all know what a nightmare that turned out to be.

Let's settle, then, on a brief, highly subjective survey of
the most consistently glamorous category of social events:
masked balls, which have a long and illustrious history dating
back to at least 1393, when Charles the Beloved, the Mad
King of France, was nearly burned to death during his Bal
des Sauvages. His costume, made of animal hair and paraf-
fin, caught fire from a torch—possibly not by accident—and
the quick-thinking Duchesse de Berry had to save him by
smothering the flames with her many skirts and crinolines.
Masked balls gained popularity during the Renaissance as a
key feature of the Carnival in Venice, which lasted for weeks
and engulfed every aspect of the city's life. In a society that
was rigidly structured around class and tradition, masquer-
ades offered a respite of democratic intermixing—not to
mention gambling, drinking, and seducing. True selves were
revealed, even as identities were concealed. "Man is least
himself when he talks in his own person," Oscar Wilde once
proclaimed. "Give him a mask, and he will tell you the truth."

That principle still applies today, and van Wyck is a
big proponent of masks in his own work. "They give you
permission to misbehave," he says. "You can be who you are
at your core without caring about the role you are forced to
play day to day." Even his sister Mimi's wedding reception in

Charleston, in 2007, was a masquerade ball; and more than six centuries after Charles the Beloved, van Wyck celebrated his fortieth birthday in 2015 with his own Bal des Sauvages. It took place not in an old-world chateau but in a windowless warehouse in Manhattan, where a mirrored vestibule featured blood-streaked walls and guests of honor included a tiger rescued from a circus and a deceptively cuddly jaguar cub.

Practically all of the grandest soirées of the twentieth century were masked balls, emblematic of an era in which entertaining was not just about marking a special occasion. Throwing a party was an end in itself—an expression of savoir faire for an ever-shrinking class of aesthetes who had the means to devote their lives to the unabashed pursuit of elegance and taste. Part social performance, theatrical happening, and free-for-all, these events also provided an important opportunity for the artists and designers of the day to develop vital relationships with an otherwise unapproachable aristocracy and haute bourgeoisie.

Consider, for example, the case of Count Étienne de Beaumont, a Parisian dandy who prided himself in spotting up-and-comers—be they painters, musicians, writers, or socialites—and amplifying their talents. De Beaumont, a renowned patron of the arts and key supporter of Sergei Diaghilev's Ballets Russes, practically gave a ball a year for over two decades—each time commissioning artistic sets, costumes, and stage designs that would be used for one night only. (A quick sampling: the Tales of Perrault Ball, the Games Ball, the Louis XIV Ball, the Opera Entrances Ball, the Famous Paintings Ball, the Racine Tricentenary Ball, the Kings and Queens Ball . . .) That's without even mentioning his Soirées de Paris, a mix of music hall, ballet, poetry, and theater that he organized in tandem with art luminaries such as Jean Cocteau, Georges Braque, Pablo Picasso, and Erik Satie at La Cigale theater, starting in 1924.

Marie-Laure de Noailles and her husband, Charles, were also among the biggest supporters of the arts in their day. They underwrote Jean Cocteau's film *The Blood of a Poet* and Luis Buñuel's surrealist masterpiece *The Andalusian Dog*. The latter, with scenes including a razor cutting into an eyeball and a man dressed in nuns' clothes, was considered so scandalous that for a moment it seemed like the couple would be socially ostracized and excommunicated from the Catholic Church. But rather than retreat or apologize, Marie-Laure and Charles doubled down in their support of the avant-garde, which would continue until Marie-Laure's death in 1970. Villa Noailles, the house they commissioned from Robert Mallet-Stevens in Hyères, in the south of France, is now considered one of the best examples of International Style architecture. And their Materials Ball, held in 1929, remains an artistic highlight of that era. All costumes had to be fashioned using materials other than fabric, such as cardboard, cellophane, or paper. The composer Francis Poulenc created a concerto for piano and eighteen instruments, the choreographer Bronislava Nijinska oversaw dance performances, and lanterns projected drawings by Jean Hugo. Guests included Max Ernst, Louis Aragon, and Salvador Dalí.

Many assumed that World War II would put an end to the golden era of costume balls, but in 1951, as if to sweep away any intrusive thoughts of Marshall Plan–era austerity, Carlos de Beistegui, a Mexican-born plutocrat who had studied at Eton and settled in Paris, invited two thousand of "the world's most blue-blooded and/or richest inhabitants," as *Life* magazine described them, to celebrate the restoration of the Palazzo Labia in Venice, which he had purchased three years prior. Plans for his housewarming, which was said to cost half a billion francs at a time when Europe was still in ruins, were panned as a moral indecency; to quell any protests, de Beistegui, with an imperial wave of his checkbook, gave the mayor of Venice 200 million francs for "popular entertainments" all over the city. Bigwigs— and big wigs—arrived at Palazzo Labia by gondola or motorboat, sometimes standing, on account of their opulent getups, and were screened by a private detective in period clothes. It is said that Pierre Cardin's career was made that evening, thanks to the thirty or so ensembles he created. Christian Dior and Salvador Dalí collaborated on their outfits, and de Beistegui changed six times, according to *Life*. One costume was, appropriately, of a Venetian doge; but the most memorable image of that evening was de Beistegui in scarlet robes, wearing a cascading curly wig and sixteen-inch platform shoes that made him nearly seven feet tall.

De Beistegui may have been the king—or doge—of his social set, but of all the bon vivants of the postwar era, it was Alexis von Rosenberg, Baron de Redé, who raised the most eyebrows. The baron started his adult life as a kept man, a fact that he never denied. He was the scion of a prominent banking dynasty, but his mother died of leukemia in 1931, when de Redé was nine, and his father committed suicide eight years later, after going bankrupt. The young de Redé made his way from Zurich, where he was born, to Los Angeles and New York, and at the age of nineteen he met the Chilean-born Arturo López-Willshaw, who had made an enormous fortune in guano fertilizer, otherwise known as bird droppings. Eventually, de Redé moved in with López-Willshaw, who was twenty years his senior, and his wife, Patricia, settling in their Versailles-esque property in Neuilly, on the outskirts of Paris. ("I was not in love," he famously said of the arrangement. "But I needed protection, and I was aware that he could provide this.") The three of them would often appear together at balls and other social engagements, but at the end of the night López-Willshaw and de Redé would repair to a palatial apartment in the Hôtel Lambert, a seventeenth-century hôtel particulier in the heart of Paris owned by social stalwarts Guy and Marie-Hélène de Rothschild. Patricia headed back to Neuilly, where she was free to pursue her own romantic entanglements.

López-Willshaw died in 1962, and his vast wealth was divided between his wife and lover. De Redé did not rest on his laurels: he became a partner in a bank, invested in art, and oversaw the Rolling Stones' financial portfolio. But that was not what made him famous. A consummate taste-maker, he decorated his rooms at the Hôtel Lambert in red and gold and became a modern-day saloniste, described by many of his contemporaries as the best host in Europe. He befriended all the swells of his time, including the Duke and Duchess of Windsor, Brigitte Bardot, Yves Saint Laurent, and Elizabeth Taylor and Richard Burton.

In 1969, de Redé gave a Bal Oriental at the Hôtel Lambert, which made news across continents. "An enchanting reprise of the great costume balls held in Paris in the seventeenth and eighteenth centuries," is how *Vogue* described it, noting that de Redé had hired live extras dressed as characters in a Veronese fresco to lean over a balcony and applaud as his friends arrived, while Indian musicians serenaded them on zithers, flutes, and drums. Also of interest to the magazine was a jeweled and turbaned maharaja who accessorized his robes with a hand-carried lion cub; another guest, outfitted like a mogul hunter, sported a large falcon on his wrist. Sadly, there was no reporting on whether the two creatures became acquainted later on at the salon that had been converted into "a discotheque with a gold-starred blue ceiling, low divans strewn with Turkish cushions around the dance floor, and alcoves lined in red velvet, dimly illuminated by multi-colored Turkish lamps."

De Redé was Marie-Hélène de Rothschild's greatest ally, and a few years later it was her turn to make a statement. Marie-Hélène Naila Stephanie Josina van Zuylen van Nyevelt van de Haar had added de Rothschild to her not inconsiderable list of surnames when she married her third cousin, Baron Guy de Rothschild, at a time when the de Rothschild banking family presided over what was thought to be the greatest private fortune on earth. Guy and Marie Hélène's country pile was the Château de Ferrières, which boasted eighty guest rooms, thirty square kilometers of forest, and a 120-foot-long central hall. It was not a shabby setting for a Surrealist Ball.

And so, in December 1972, after deciphering an invitation written backward so that it had to be read using a mirror, guests were greeted at Ferrières, which was lit with moving floodlights to create the effect that it was on fire, by footmen dressed as cats. Dinner table centerpieces consisted of taxidermy turtles, doll heads, and high-heeled shoes; charger plates were covered in fur, and napkins had lips. Standout dishes included an "imbroglio of exquisite corpses," "extra-lucid soup," and "peaches and goat cheese screaming with sadness"; dessert was served on a mannequin corpse resting on a bed of roses. De Rothschild wore a stag head crying real diamond tears, and de Redé an elaborate headpiece created by Salvador Dalí that depicted various faces in one.

By the mid to late 1970s, with the disco era in full swing, such elaborate evenings, with their emphasis on nobility and old money, started to feel antiquated. To be sure, their influence was still felt, but as new players entered the social scene, the events that made news were far less stuffy. In 1977, for example, when the Yves Saint Laurent accessories designer and all-around muse Loulou de la Falaise married Thadée Klossowski, son of the painter Balthus, she eschewed a traditional wedding dress in favor of white harem pants, gold sandals, and a feathered turban. For the nuptial festivities, where punkettes commingled with style mavens dressed up to the nines, de la Falaise changed into a shimmering blue dress with a headpiece of stars and a crescent moon. The journalist Joan Juliet Buck, who would eventually go on to become the editor of French *Vogue*, intimated that well-wishers had partaken in more than a congratulatory glass of champagne. "A certain kind of manic ecstasy keeps verbal exchanges short, table-hopping constant, and spirits high," she wrote of the occasion.

It's telling of this changing of the guard that, as impeccably produced as the aristocratic European balls were, the gathering that most captured the popular imagination around that time was Truman Capote's Black and White

Ball, inspired by the famous Ascot scene in *My Fair Lady* and held at the Plaza Hotel in Manhattan. There is a simple and very good reason why it is so well known and so often referenced: knowingly or not, Capote created the template for today's celebrity-obsessed parties.

In 1966, Capote was at the peak of his literary and social powers, having just published *In Cold Blood*, a nonfiction novel about four murders in the town of Holcomb, Kansas. The book made him more famous, at least for a while, than pretty much any other American author: he was on the covers of *Newsweek*, *Saturday Review*, *Book Week*, and the *New York Times Book Review*, and was the subject of *Life* magazine's longest profile ever published about a writer. After all was said and done, his windfall from the book totaled around $2 million. Capote was the toast of New York and became a favorite of the society doyennes he called his swans: Babe Paley, Marella Agnelli, Lee Radziwill, Slim Keith, C. Z. Guest, and Gloria Guinness.

He was, understandably, in a mood to celebrate. Capote announced to anyone with ears that he was planning a bash to which he would invite "everyone"—by which he meant 480 meticulously selected guests. (As the date approached, the number grew to 540; the Plaza's Grand Ballroom could accommodate a maximum of 550.) To preempt social snip-ing, Capote shrewdly gave the party not for himself but in honor of the only woman who could hover above his swans: Katharine Graham, who had recently become the publisher of the *Washington Post*, following her husband's suicide in 1963.

For months, Capote scribbled names in his black-and-white composition notebook, adding some and crossing out others as he gossiped and conferred with those at the top of the list. Pretty soon it became clear to New York society that anyone who wasn't invited might as well be dead—in some cases, literally. An acquaintance of Capote's who had not yet received an invitation told him that his wife had threatened to kill herself if they didn't attend; Capote acquiesced, perhaps mindful that his own mother had committed suicide. Others who hadn't made the cut left New York, feigning prior obligations. Such was the hysteria regarding who was or wasn't invited that after the ball, to the enormous chagrin of those who had skipped town, the *New York Times* published Capote's full guest list—an honor that was usually reserved for state dinners at the White House.

The actual invitees included most of the boldface names

that were to be expected, including Capote's swans, Andy Warhol, Frank Sinatra, Mia Farrow, Tallulah Bankhead, Diana Vreeland, and Oscar de la Renta. But for Capote, the event was also a sort of social experiment in which he brought together people with different interests and from different walks of life. That concept, any event planner will tell you today, has become obvious; but at the time it felt revolutionary. That's why American royalty like Gloria Vanderbilt could rub elbows with the unprepossessing documentary filmmaker Albert Maysles, and why actual royalty, like the Maharani of Jaipur or the Italian princess Luciana Pignatelli (wearing a borrowed sixty-carat Harry Winston diamond), could hang out with the economist John Kenneth Galbraith, who according to reports from the time danced "like a hepcat" to Peter Duchin's orchestra. Capote also welcomed eleven of the small-town friends he'd made in Kansas while researching *In Cold Blood*, as well as Katharine Graham's secretary, one of his former schoolteachers, and a doorman from the UN Plaza, the building where he had just bought an apartment. Equally noteworthy was that he openly received his lover of many years, Jack Dunphy, as well as members of Dunphy's family.

"I have always observed, in almost every situation, and I have been in almost every situation, that people tend to cling to their own types," Capote told *Esquire* magazine. "The very rich people, for instance, tend to like the company of very rich people. The international social set likes international socialites. Writers writers, artists artists. I have thought for years that it would be interesting to bring these different people together and see what happens."

He also believed in bringing together 450 bottles of Taittinger champagne with scrambled eggs, sausages, biscuits, spaghetti and meatballs, and chicken hash, which is what was served at midnight. (It's possible that not everyone indulged: Capote had strong-armed friends into hosting several pre-ball dinners all over town to further heighten anticipation.) The decorations were sparse: candles, balloons, and red tablecloths to inject color. And while many of the guests vied to outdo one another with their disguises—Halston designed a white zibeline mask with a faux ruby for Babe Paley, and a pink mink bunny number for Candice Bergen (which, incidentally, she wore again decades later to van Wyck's Bal des Sauvages)—Capote was happy to reveal that his own mask had been purchased at FAO Schwarz for thirty-nine cents.

Capote once joked that he was a better publicist than writer; one might add that he was an even better party planner. According to Curt Gathje, the Plaza's historian, the Black and White Ball generated more press coverage than the Beatles when they had stayed at the hotel two years prior. With a relatively modest investment—the ball was said to have cost $16,000—Capote had successfully saturated the media, boosted sales of his books, and extended the buzz surrounding him for years to come. It explains why that evening has been revisited so many times. Princess Yasmin Aga Khan hosted a black-and-white fete in 1991 to commemorate the twenty-fifth anniversary of the original; Puff Daddy threw his own black-and-white bash in 1998; Christie's also attempted to re-create it in 2006; and in 2019, Ralph Lauren held a fashion show in which the singer Janelle Monáe performed in a halter-neck tuxedo dress, and all guests were asked to wear—you guessed it—black and white.

Capote understood that celebrations could be about far more than expressions of goodwill. They could be monetized and strategically deployed for targeted purposes. In the decades that followed, events ranging from bar mitzvahs to charity benefits to corporate shindigs would become increasingly over the top. And unlike the time of Étienne de Beaumont or Baron de Redé, most people in the late twentieth century didn't have the leisure, discipline, or, in many cases, taste to pull them off themselves. That's how event planning, a profession that had previously never been quite articulated as such, finally came into existence.

CHAPTER SIX

——

Once the formality of European nobility became largely a thing of the past, a different pecking order was formed as the old social guard jostled for supremacy with fashion designers, "it" girls, artists, full-time party-goers, and a new-money elite. Who cared about fancy titles, secluded country estates, and stiff manners when you could go out and meet a new cast of characters every night? Discos, not ballrooms, became the new performative spaces.

The embodiment of this scene was Studio 54 in New York, with its confluence of glamour, celebrity, money, and sex. Although it was only open for thirty-three months, from 1977 to 1980, Studio 54 transformed nightlife forever. Countless movies and books have chronicled the shenanigans that took place at the club, with its shirtless busboys in short shorts, balconies for casual sex, abundance of cocaine, and dingy VIP basement where anything went. Understandably, these accounts tend to focus either on celebrity regulars like Halston, Liza Minnelli, and Andy Warhol, or on the cautionary tale of its founders, Steve Rubell and Ian Schrager, who were arrested for tax evasion when the police finally raided and shut down the club. But there is one important element that always seems to be overlooked, or taken for granted: the dramatic physical transformations that the space regularly underwent.

Studio 54 operated in an old theater complete with movable sets and stage lights; ahead of their time, Rubell and Schrager hired design experts to continuously zhoosh things up and create novel nocturnal amusements. The fashion designer Valentino celebrated his birthday there with a circus-themed party that included a ring, trapezes, and costumes straight out of Fellini's film *The Clowns*; when Dolly Parton visited, she was ushered into a disco farm complete with chickens, horses, donkeys, and bales of hay. That made Bianca Jagger's famous birthday bash, in which she strode into the club atop a white stallion, feel casual by comparison.

It was in this heady atmosphere—try getting a permit today for livestock in a nightclub—that a young upstart named Robert Isabell cut his teeth. The son of a power company lineman, Isabell was a twenty-six-year-old florist working in Minneapolis when he moved to New York in 1978. On his first night in town he happened to walk by Studio 54 and approached to investigate what all the commotion on the street was about. Probably because of his wholesome good looks, he was plucked from the crowd and ushered inside by Rubell, who stood guard at the door every night to literally decide who was in and out.

Isabell didn't waste his chance. He soon landed a job with Renny Reynolds, a florist whose clients included Studio 54, and then started working for Schrager and Rubell, designing the decor for special events at the club. One occasion in particular made his reputation—for New Year's Eve, Isabell dumped four tons of glitter on the dance floor, covering it four or five inches deep and creating the impression, as Schrager later recalled, that everyone was walking on stardust. Weeks later it was possible to know who had been at Studio 54 that night because of the shimmering specks that had infiltrated people's wardrobes and homes.

(Things have a way of coming around full circle. More than forty years later, van Wyck threw a quinceañera party for Schrager's daughter Ava. He covered the floor with two thousand pounds of violet glitter and used the original Studio 54 lighting rig, which Schrager had kept in storage.)

It was in the 1980s, however, that the event planning industry truly took off. Anyone who has seen movies like *Wall Street*, *The Bonfire of the Vanities*, and *Working Girl* knows there was a simple reason: money. The stock market was on fire, and its overlords were eager to flaunt their wealth. The Nouvelle Society, as these Wall Street types and their wives came to be known, became regulars on the charity circuit; to burnish their reputations, they pounced on galas thrown by highbrow, traditional institutions like the American Ballet Theatre and the Metropolitan Museum of Art's Costume Institute. (Yes, that's the same party that is now considered "The Oscars of Fashion" for its abundance of celebrities in Instagram-friendly outfits.) The Nouvelle Society's ethos has been compared to that of pre-revolutionary France, and with good reason. Even the sartorial choices of this set, characterized by entrance-making Christian Lacroix "pouf" dresses so voluminous that they kept their wearers at an arm's length from their escorts, brought to mind the excesses of Versailles.

Isabell set the template for the modern event planner because he was savvy enough to capitalize on both the private and public needs of his clients. One night he could be overseeing a fundraiser for the Municipal Art Society; the next, a lavish wedding for Whitney Houston. (His repertoire wasn't limited to celebratory occasions, as he proved in 1994, when he quietly organized Jacqueline Kennedy Onassis's funeral.) Isabell understood what Manhattan's upper crust knew all too well: that in order to make money, you needed to spend money. In an era of conspicuous consumption and round-the-clock socializing, organizations started to rely heavily on splashy benefits to cover their operating funds rather than on plain old boring donations. It was imperative to create experiences that people would remember—not an easy task in New York—so that the process could be successfully repeated the following year. The rule of thumb was simple. Expenses were around 25 percent of the gross; to make a million dollars, you had to spend $250,000.

Even so, the most lucrative events were still private ones, thrown by clients who had plenty of peers to impress but none to answer to. Chief among them was the financier Saul Steinberg and his third wife, Gayfryd, who was often referred to as the queen of Nouvelle Society. The Steinbergs lived in a thirty-four-room triplex apartment on Park Avenue that once belonged to John D. Rockefeller, packed with eighteenth- and nineteenth-century French and English furniture and hung with a collection of old master paintings. Those artworks, in fact, were the inspiration for one of the decade's most talked-about bashes, which was both praised and derided for its extravagance.

To help Saul celebrate his fiftieth birthday in 1988, Isabell re-created a seventeenth-century Flemish drinking hall in the Steinbergs' Quogue, Long Island, estate. That would have been par for the course those days, except that it was enlivened with ten tableaux vivants inspired by the businessman's favorite paintings. Just in case something was lost in translation: museum-worthy masterpieces, such as Rembrandt's *Danaë*, in which Perseus's mother is depicted nude as she awaits Zeus, were re-created in human scale using live actors inside framed vitrines. The gossip columnist Liz Smith later described the crowd that night as "A-list nouveau riche and rising," and recalled surreal moments such as coming upon identical twins posed as mermaids in the pool and spotting a Vermeer girl dancing with a movie studio executive during her break from tableau vivant duty.

Isabell didn't have the field to himself. Philip Baloun, another florist who also trained under Renny Reynolds, opened his own firm in 1979 and landed major clients such as the New York Botanical Garden, for which he organized yearly orchid shows, and George Soros, for whom he once built a life-size Hungarian town square as a tribute to his birthplace. Baloun's obituary—he died of cancer in 2007—stated that his prices started at "around $30,000 for a simple affair for which he provided flowers and décor," to as much as $10 million, presumably for something not the slightest bit simple. No word on the price tag for the evening he once organized for a visiting Prince Charles in Lincoln Center Plaza, where Baloun conjured a forest with real trees inside an enormous tent with a midnight-blue ceiling decorated with stars.

Over on the West Coast, Stanlee Gatti would, in time, be dubbed "the Bay Area's answer to Robert Isabell" by *W* magazine. Gatti grew up in the tiny New Mexico town of Raton, which, it is safe to say, was not a hotbed of glamour, given that *ratón* means mouse in Spanish. Gatti arrived in San Francisco in 1978, at age twenty-one, with $750 in his pocket and started working at the St. Francis Hotel. He swiftly rose to the position of hospitality director, which meant he got to deal with VIP guests such as Yves Saint Laurent and Queen Elizabeth, who visited in 1983. He got his break in 1985, when the San Francisco Symphony hired him to organize its seventy-fifth anniversary gala. Gatti took a risk and broke with the institution's genteel traditions by decorating the party venue in shades of bright red, orange, and hot pink. The very next morning he knew the gamble had paid off—clients started coming out of the woodwork, and soon he had his own business with supporters that included local grand dames like the philanthropist Ann Getty and the writer Danielle Steel.

Baloun, Gatti, and other event planners—Preston Bailey, Colin Cowie, David Monn, and David Stark, to name just four—had or continue to have full, successful careers spanning decades. (Gatti was appointed president of the San Francisco Arts Commission in 1996 and is close with California governor Gavin Newsom.) Raúl Àvila, who apprenticed as Isabell's assistant, has been responsible for the Met Gala since 2007, and also handles the Tony Awards festivities. Still, none of them has achieved the same name recognition as Isabell. This is perhaps due to the ability that Isabell had to adapt to changing mores—or at least to his ability to *project* the idea of change—especially after the stock market crashed in 1987 and the go-go eighties gave way to the less ostentatious nineties.

"It's important to word things more carefully these days,"

Isabell told a *New York Times* reporter who visited him at home in 1996. "That's why the word 'understated' works so well in the 90s." By then, Isabell had moved into a three-story town house in downtown Manhattan that he had bought almost as a ruin and renovated to exacting specifications. It didn't have a proper kitchen—why should he have bothered with one if he never ate in—but boasted, among other amenities, a glass bridge suspended over a jungle-like, sixty-five-foot-high atrium, a sound system with forty-eight speakers, and a floating staircase that was often accented with votive candles. "It's about looking at things in a simplified way," Isabell added, without a hint of irony.

Isabell's notions of simplicity and understatement were decidedly relative, and not just when it came to his living quarters. The previous year, one of his key clients at the time, Marie-Chantal Miller, daughter of the duty-free tycoon Robert Miller, had married Prince Pavlos of Greece in England. Isabell organized a welcome dinner for the wedding party at a country estate outside of London and installed so many lights in the adjoining fields that Heathrow Airport had to be notified for fear that his atmospheric flourishes might be mistaken for a runway by incoming airplanes.

Nonetheless, in addition to the glitzy Millers, Isabell worked with a remarkable range of clients. These included nonprofits like Bette Midler's New York Restoration Project; paragons of minimalism such as Calvin Klein and Philip Johnson; fashion figures led by the *Vogue* editor Anna Wintour, who was just starting to jazz up the Costume Institute Gala at the Met; corporate behemoths including IBM, for which Isabell decorated its Manhattan headquarters; and political figures like the Clintons, who hired him to handle Christmas decorations at the White House. Isabell's genius lay in his ability to strike the perfect tone to match the sensibilities of each client. A good party planner is not unlike a therapist, who listens to and deciphers what people need or want, even if they can't quite articulate it themselves.

As Isabell became almost as well known as some of his clients, he began seeking out other ventures. The first was the most obvious for someone who had started out as a florist: a line of fragrances made from essential oils that he launched in 1996 and named Perfumes Isabell. There were high hopes for the project but, impetuously, Isabell went against conventional marketing wisdom and launched five products all at once. The gambit was a flop, and the short-lived company folded. Isabell pivoted to real estate, emboldened by the successful renovation of his house and Manhattan's skyrocketing housing prices. He acquired a couple of buildings in Manhattan's Meatpacking District but soon wanted more. In 2006, at the peak of the market, he gambled everything he had on a $45 million property that he intended to convert into a studio building for photographers and other creatives, but he struggled to secure the necessary city permits. Isabell died of a heart attack a year later, heavily leveraged and with dwindling prospects.

Coincidentally or not, van Wyck's star was on the rise as Isabell's was dimming. There was plenty of work to go around in the late nineties and early aughts—the film, fashion, and luxury industries were going global, and designers were constantly staking out new ground with over-the-top events and presentations. Houses like Dior, Valentino, and Gucci set up camp in Los Angeles during awards season, dressing the stars of the moment. Red carpet openings and after-parties began to double as fashion catwalks. And soon enough, big corporations started craving the kind of buzz that these affairs could generate.

CHAPTER SEVEN

A round 2003, the American division of Mercedes-Benz hired van Wyck to produce almost all of its events worldwide and put his company under contract. It was the beginning of a big shift: in addition to high-profile social supporters, van Wyck was able to develop a solid roster of corporate clients, too. "Once Mercedes came on board we were able to really plan ahead for the first time," van Wyck says. "All of a sudden you take a business that is basically freelance, where you're going from project to project, you hopefully have a calendar for the following three, six, and nine months—but you may not—and you give it stability. That's when we started developing a proper full-time staff. And it was great for Mercedes, too, because we could think about their events holistically, reuse all kinds of props and branded materials, and achieve significant economies of scale for them."

Soon after that, other big names came calling. Van Wyck was asked to oversee the opening of Hearst Tower in 2006, a project that was not only huge but hugely symbolic: the building, designed by Norman Foster, was the first skyscraper to break ground in New York City after 9/11. "We were hired to plan about ten events over the course of eleven months, culminating in a big sort of Cirque du Soleil–type performance and a Stevie Wonder concert in the atrium of the tower," van Wyck recalls. "We were dealing with an extremely rigorous corporate organization, so we had to hire a whole new team in order to service a client like that. The Hearst Tower project really enabled us to expand our local staff, because the Mercedes events were all over the world, but this was all in New York, and it was a lot. We got to a point where we were having to say no to other jobs because we simply didn't have enough resources."

The financial collapse of 2008, which happened just a couple of years after that, was disastrous for event planners as a whole. No one was in the mood to take economic risks, let alone flaunt disposable income at a time when businesses were going bankrupt and people across the country were losing their homes and being laid off. "Everything just

stopped," van Wyck recalls. "It was a crazy time because no one knew how low the market was going to go . . . ten percent, thirty percent, fifty percent? As soon as you know you can adjust, make plans, re-budget, reallocate, and get on with it. But in the meantime, it was like the gears of the machine had just frozen. People give events for a lot of reasons—to express gratitude, to show love, to celebrate milestones—but they don't give them to make other people feel bad, and for a moment celebrating took on an almost negative sociopolitical aspect, where you were a jerk to be seen having fun. We didn't get a single call from the day Lehman Brothers collapsed, in September of 2008, until the end of February."

The irony is that although the financial crisis completely wiped out many in his industry—van Wyck estimates that around 30 percent of his competitors went out of business—2009 turned out to be one of his company's best years. He considers that time an inflection point in his career. "We knew we had no control over how individuals wanted to engage socially on a personal level," van Wyck says. "But we were certain that we could still deliver value to companies. So we pivoted and focused on them, explaining that we had to create new ways to reach their customers through very strategic events."

Van Wyck remembers the launch of a jewelry brand's latest collection, which had been scheduled for December

2008 well before the stock market cratered. The typical scenario for this type of thing, he explained, was that you would create a beautiful setting in the store, make individual appointments with collectors and journalists, explain the craftsmanship of the pieces, and then wait and see over the next week or so how sales went. "At this time no one even wanted to carry a shopping bag," van Wyck says. "Who would have wanted to be seen out and about buying, of all things, jewels that cost hundreds of thousands of dollars?" Van Wyck's solution was not to cancel the presentation or scale it down, but rather to work with his client to create an altogether different kind of event. "I said, we are not cutting expenses, we are doubling down, because this is our only shot, and this is what we are going to do: We are concerned about the customers not wanting to come to the boutique? Then we are going to bring the boutique to the customers."

Van Wyck was not oblivious to the fact that the idea of spending considerable resources promoting jewelry at a time of need could have rankled people. But there are two sides to a coin. "When money changes hands there is a multiplier effect on its value in the economy," van Wyck says. "So if people who have money don't spend it, people who need money can't make money—carpenters, makeup artists, waiters, porters . . . precisely those who have to be paid most urgently. In a time of crisis, no social good comes from telling someone with inert capital not to deploy it."

And so, instead of the three hundred or so people that would have normally attended the jewelry showing, the list was edited down to key customers, along with a few Oscar-caliber actors like Meryl Streep and Glenn Close, and magazine editors in chief. The jewels were inspired by gardens, so van Wyck commandeered the ground floor of the Plaza Hotel and sodded it with a carpet of grass, brought in trees and plants, and created a French topiary garden, an Italian herb garden, an English rose garden, and a Japanese water garden.

"Guests came to experience all of these environments, everyone sat in a different area, and everything around you referenced the theme. Based on where you were sitting, your table was different—if you were in the Italian garden, for example, it was covered in Fortuny fabrics and damasks," van Wyck says. "Then we had a series of performances: a French ballerina, an Italian opera singer, Japanese shadow dancers . . . and with each act, the performers wore more and more jewelry. At the end, for the finale, a beautiful woman came out completely naked except for the most incredible jewels you'd ever seen."

Sounds like a nice night out, but what about sales? As the performances were taking place, handlers brought out the jewelry on trays and exhibited it from table to table. "People were having the surreal feeling of being in an Edwardian hotel from 1907, but they were also in a garden, being entertained by incredibly talented performers, and seeing the finest examples of the artistry of jewel-making in the world," van Wyck says. "They were able to touch the necklaces and bracelets and try them on, but they were all one of a kind, so if you liked something and you saw so-and-so eyeing it, you wanted to get it for yourself as soon as you could. At the culmination of the evening, after everyone had been drinking and having delicious food, they wanted to take home with them the magical feeling they had experienced, so we brought out the credit card machines, and we let them take the magic home by taking the jewelry home." Van Wyck's client sold millions of dollars' worth of jewelry that night. "That experiment made us realize that we could bring a brand to life through experiences that could almost instantly have a measurable effect on how people felt about a product."

Three months after the bejeweled garden party, van Wyck convinced the Guggenheim Museum not only to allow him to host a Mercedes-Benz launch there, but also to remove several windowpanes from the building's façade in order to insert the latest luxury car into its iconic circular atrium. "We sold three Maybachs that night," van Wyck says. But that immediate gain, while certainly welcome, was only part of the goal. "What we were and are always trying to do is make people love the brands we represent. If you need a product you will buy it, but if you *love* a product you will buy it and then you'll tell everyone you know about it. At an event for three hundred, you're reaching three hundred people directly—but if they talk to their friends, then you've amplified the message exponentially. We were at the vanguard of using events to build authentic connections with people who had an affinity with a brand. Then you could nourish those connections into real relationships."

That might sound like circuitous marketing jibber-jabber, but van Wyck is actually describing a substantial shift in his business: purposely or not, he was becoming a de facto marketing consultant. "At that time, some corporate clients were laying off people in their events departments, so they would come to us and say, we need to make this happen, how do we do it?" Van Wyck was happy to oblige, and his role became even more crucial in the years that followed, as social media accelerated the migration of companies' marketing budgets from traditional advertising to digital and experiential campaigns. Real-life events satisfied the need for public human interaction that had been diminished by social media; in turn, they provided content for the very platforms that made those in-person interactions optional to begin with. Magazine and newspaper ads dwindled as brands generated their own content and reallocated resources to promote it using influencers.

In 2016 van Wyck officially split the company in two and launched Workshop, catering specifically to brand experiences and communications. Van Wyck oversees both Workshop and Van Wyck & Van Wyck, but they have different partners and management structures. Workshop tends to produce bigger events, but Van Wyck & Van Wyck often has more to juggle. "An entire quarter for Workshop can be made by one event, if we are working, for example, on the Super Bowl," he says. "But in the summer Van Wyck & Van Wyck can produce four high-profile weddings. So the workload and revenue kind of even out."

The difference between the sister companies, though, is about more than just scale. "When a company gives an event, that's an investment," van Wyck says. "They are spending funds over which they exercise a fiduciary responsibility, so that really has to be considered. You are becoming part of their business plan and there is a real expectation of returns. Sometimes we have to say to a client, that's a great idea, but it's not a good investment. Sales events, for example, work really well when you have high-unit-cost items, like fine jewelry, or a $400,000 car—in those cases, one event can pay for itself many times over. But if you're selling a forty-dollar video game, you'd better have a great social media and online strategy—otherwise you are leaving money on the table."

Now that brands have become content generators, their events need to be specifically tailored to incentivize guests to share their messaging, especially on digital platforms. "There is an opportunity for us to reach more audiences than ever before," van Wyck says. "A handful of people with large social followings could have a bigger impact than a seated dinner for two hundred." That's why when you attend a movie premiere, benefit auction, or fashion party nowadays, you are bound to find a step-and-repeat accessible not just to celebrities but to anyone with a smartphone. And making sure that backgrounds will pop on Instagram is now a requirement when planning pretty much any kind of branded event. "Often, you feel like the entire world is watching," van Wyck says. "You have to create moments at a party that are not just for the invited guests."

A good example of this phenomenon is the evolution of fashion shows. In the pre-digital era, they were subdued, intimate affairs: journalists and store buyers would be invited to presentations where twenty or thirty models would strut down a runway showcasing a designer's newest offerings. Everyone else had to wait three to six months to see what the clothes actually looked like, once they appeared in magazines or were delivered to the stores. But with the advent of style websites—and later, platforms like Facebook and Instagram—it became possible for viewers all over the world to judge the collections for themselves immediately. On a computer or phone screen, however, clothes alone aren't always enough to create a viral moment. So fashion shows started becoming major events, like one-off plays or short movies, complete with one-of-a-kind sets, celebrity guest stars, multimillion-dollar budgets, and drones filming overhead.

Two names stand out in the fashion event planning field: Etienne Russo and Alexandre de Betak. Russo is based in Brussels and got his start working as a model and all-around odd-job guy for the Belgian designer Dries Van Noten; he wound up producing Van Noten's first show, in 1990, and never looked back. At that time, going the extra mile might have entailed covering a catwalk with grass, or securing a beautiful historical building as the venue for a presentation. By contrast, Russo's more recent productions have included, to name but a few, installing a rocket that simulated takeoff inside the Grand Palais in Paris as a Chanel show ended; suspending eighty-ton, three-hundred-foot-long blocks of ice from railroad tracks for Hugo Boss; and creating the illusion that a dancer was trapped inside an immobile white plaster curtain for Maison Margiela.

De Betak, for his part, is the Paris-based mastermind behind Dior's famously astonishing performances, from John Galliano's customized "Diorient Express" train, from which models emerged at the Gare d'Austerlitz in Paris, and which helped the designer skyrocket to fame, to a more recent presentation held inside a mirror-clad box in Moscow's Red Square. For the Italian label Berluti, de Betak once made men's shoes float through the air, held aloft by large white balloons, in the ornate halls of the Musée des Arts Décoratifs in Paris. It's unlikely that anyone remembers exactly what the wingtips and brogues looked like, but you can be sure that no one who was there soon forgot the energy of that moment. The challenge for Russo and de Betak nowadays—as well as for van Wyck, who has plenty of fashion accounts himself, and for any other event planner who works with luxury clients—is to somehow be simultaneously inclusive and exclusive, maintaining a sense of mystery while also taking into consideration an ever-expanding digital audience.

Still, for all of these historical and technological shifts, van Wyck believes that the core of what he does, "the delivery of hospitality," is always fundamentally the same, regardless of the medium. "Humans are highly evolved beings, but we all still have a primal, basic need to be included, to belong," he says. "Events are an opportunity to use those primal needs as a way to get into the minds of people in a positive way. If they feel good, they will want to come back."

This happens organically in private parties, which are about love, happiness, fun, and celebration. What van Wyck aims to do with his business events is generate those same kinds of emotions, but in order to build a foundation for engagement, persuasion, and content creation. "You associate that positive, satisfied feeling of having a great time and being appreciated with something else, whether it's jewelry or a car, that under regular circumstances might not evoke that type of response," he says. "At Workshop, we still use all the traditional elements of a Van Wyck and Van Wyck party—we just do it with a specific, measurable goal in mind."

CHAPTER EIGHT

A few months after his parents' fiftieth anniversary, I was looking forward to accompanying van Wyck to a Workshop event. The reopening of the Ritz-Carlton hotel in Miami was going to be a splashy affair, and I was eager to see how everything I had witnessed van Wyck do in the private realm translated into a corporate setting. Unfortunately, I never got the chance. The grand unveiling was slated for April 2020—a time during which, as we all know, the Covid-19 pandemic was wreaking havoc all over the world. Everyone was in lockdown.

"I've been outlawed," van Wyck said with wry humor when I spoke to him on the phone during quarantine. "I don't consider myself a terribly conventional person, but I never thought my entire oeuvre would be illegal." He was referring, of course, to the social distancing rules that had been mandated in order to avoid the spread of contagion. New Yorkers were struggling with the restrictions but were resigned to the fact that they would be living with some version of them for the foreseeable future. The mood was about as far from festive as could be and begged an obvious question: If people weren't even supposed to visit close friends and family, and big celebrations were, as van Wyck had correctly pointed out, quite literally against the law, what on earth was he going to do?

"The current situation is completely devastating for a business like ours," van Wyck acknowledged. "The first few days after we were all told to stay home were actually quite busy, because we had to talk to all our clients to postpone their events and make alternate plans for what we had been working on." After that, there was nothing. Van Wyck focused on securing access to the government's businesses support program so he could sustain his payroll. "There were two weeks where I had to furlough the staff, before that loan came through," he said.

Like many others who were shocked to discover how ill-prepared the federal government was to deal with the health crisis, van Wyck and his team took matters into their own hands. He sent all the sewing machines in the warehouse to the seamstresses' homes, and his staff started making face coverings and gowns using whatever fabrics were available, including curtains, napkins, and tent ceilings. "Their work has made me so proud, especially because even when we went into furlough everyone volunteered and kept on going—they weren't getting paid but still kept sewing. Now we are back on payroll and we've made almost ten thousand masks and we have an entire system set up." The masks did not meet the necessary safety requirements for health care workers, but they proved extremely useful for people who had to interact with the public in other essential occupations. "You can wear them, for example, if you are delivering a meal to someone, or helping at a food bank," van Wyck said. The scrubs, on the other hand, could be used in medical settings. "There's a whole group of nurses at Lenox Hill Hospital who have the most beautiful English chintz gowns that were once table-cloths at a Fourth of July party we did in Southampton!"

I asked van Wyck whether he could venture a guess of more or less when he thought he might return to work. "I had a luxury fashion client ask me the other day whether we could reschedule an event for September 2020, and of course I wanted to say yes with all my heart," van Wyck said. "But I said I thought that would still be too early. Imagine if you gathered four hundred people and ten days later forty of them ended up getting sick—you would become the Typhoid Mary of the industry! You would never live that down. So I have been advising everyone to take a pause, and I think all of our clients are now on the same page."

In the meantime, the only possible approach for him, as for everyone else, was to wait and see—and to develop as many connections as possible on digital platforms. Van Wyck regularly connected with friends on Zoom but also amped his professional presence on social media. Magazines and digital publications were reaching out to tastemakers in order to generate content to try to keep their homebound audiences engaged, so van Wyck did an Instagram takeover for *Galerie* magazine and participated in a one-on-one chat with the editor in chief of *Elle Decor*, in which he revealed how to make a delicious cucumber margarita. (Try it: Peel a cucumber, purée it, and mix it with water in order to make shimmering green ice cubes. You then follow a regular margarita recipe, using 21 Seeds cucumber-and-jalapeño infused tequila—a brand that was actually developed by van Wyck—but I used regular tequila and threw in a slice of jalapeño at the end, and it was still great.) In lieu of the annual benefit for the High Line, the elevated public park in Manhattan, van Wyck hosted a Zoom chat with Martha Stewart, Diane von Furstenberg, and other supporters. During a digital fundraiser for the Cincinnati Children's

Hospital, he assured his audience that even Katy Perry gets nervous when planning a party.

I told van Wyck how disappointed I was about missing the Ritz-Carlton party, and we started discussing other Workshop projects. As it turns out, I didn't really need to worry about not having been able to go to Miami, because, without realizing it, I had already attended several Workshop events in the past. "Did you by chance go to the Longchamp opening on Fifth Avenue a couple of years ago?" van Wyck asked. "We worked on that. It was a good one." I had indeed been there and remembered it well, because there had been a line all the way around the block—not to mention, for some reason it had seemed like everyone on the streets of Midtown Manhattan was eating pastries.

Longchamp is a luxury leather goods company known for its lightweight, pliable totes. They had decided to open a big New York flagship in 2018 to coincide with their seventieth anniversary and wanted to make a splash in the city while touting their French heritage. The media strategist Vanessa von Bismarck, who works with the brand in the United States, hired Workshop to build a "Café de Longchamp," inspired by Parisian bakeries. Van Wyck's team secured permits from the mayor's office to serve coffee, espresso, croissants, éclairs, and other patisseries in front of the store for an entire week. Everything was free.

"For the opening night we brought all kinds of entertainment into the boutique, including a huge wheel of fortune where people could win different prizes or discover clues to go to other areas in the store to find something else," van Wyck said. "That alone was a big social media thing. But then, thanks to the café, instead of having an opening day, Longchamp had a whole opening week. It generated huge amounts of attention for the brand." There was plenty of foot traffic, of course, because of all the people queuing up at the café—tens of thousands of visitors, according to van Wyck. But the Café de Longchamp also became a happening of sorts, and many of the passersby who enjoyed an unexpected treat on their way to work or during their lunch break were happy to post about the experience. That, in turn, generated more real-life visitors.

There was another, even bigger event that I had attended in 2015, right around the time when van Wyck was mulling the idea of officially spinning off Workshop as a separate entity. It stuck in my mind because it was a big, lavish production, but also because no one who was there seemed to know exactly what the party was for. Even I, someone who attends a fair number of events as a magazine editor, was confounded. That, as it turned out, was part of the plan all along.

The invitation, timed for Halloween, said "Jeanne Greenberg Rohatyn & Keith Rubenstein present Lucien Smith: Macabre Suite." I knew the artist Lucien Smith and the gallerist Jeanne Greenberg Rohatyn, but I had no idea who Keith Rubenstein was. Below that were the names of six deejays and the promise of a special surprise performance. On the other side of the card there was an eclectic grouping of cohosts, including the actor Adrien Brody, the art world stalwarts Adam Lindemann and Amalia Dayan, the socialite Nicky Hilton Rothschild, the model Irina Shayk, the director Baz Luhrmann, and the businessman Ron Burkle, among many others. "The party was built around Lucien's performance and a group of hosts, top models, fashion editors, socialites, some dot-com entrepreneurs . . . interesting people that Nadine knew would draw other people," van Wyck said, referring to Nadine Johnson, one of New York's most well-connected publicists and a frequent collaborator.

There was no indication, however, of *why* any of this was taking place. And most intriguing of all was the address: a quick Google search revealed that it corresponded to an empty lot in the South Bronx, in an area along the Harlem

River known as Mott Haven. To be sure, the Bronx hadn't been the woefully neglected borough it was in the 1980s for quite some time, but I still couldn't think of a single other time when I had been invited to a big party there—let alone one featuring multiple deejays, artistic happenings, and a list of fancy guests longer than a telephone book.

I made my way uptown in a black car and upon arrival found groups of hipsters emerging from chartered school buses. It was clearly not an intimate affair. The façade of a decrepit ware-house was pulsating with green, burgundy, and purple lights. The space inside was partly open to the elements; there were bullet-shot car sculptures created by Smith, and flea market furniture scattered in makeshift rooms, at least one of which had a caved-in ceiling. In the outdoor area there were food carts from trendy eateries like Roberta's Pizza and Korilla BBQ. Bonfires, torches, and thousands of candles scattered throughout provided an eerie glow. As the evening progressed, things went from quiet and mysterious to loud to louder. Travis Scott performed, and Frankie Bones led a deejay battle. This wasn't your average polite cocktail party with announcements and toasts. It wasn't even a dance party—it was a rave.

That event, according to van Wyck, was a perfect example of why it made sense for him to make Workshop official at that time. "Think about the fact that we threw a *Halloween rave* for a very corporate client—that shows just how much the world of events had evolved by then," he said. It turns out that Keith Rubenstein, the one whose name I hadn't recognized on the invitation, wasn't an art world player or a fashion or Hollywood impresario, as many might have assumed, but a property developer. He owned the lot where everyone danced and watched the artistic performances and dined at the many stands that had been hired that night. He had also purchased several other surrounding lots and buildings and planned to convert them all into apartments. "Keith said to Nadine and me: 'Make something happen up there,'" van Wyck recalled. "We could've given people more information with the invitation, but we purposely didn't want to. The traditional launch of a real estate venture is typically a very different kind of party, and that was not what we wanted."

About three thousand people attended, but some were of special interest. "The key to the whole thing was that Nadine had invited forty guests who had more than a million followers each on Instagram," van Wyck said, citing the likes of Naomi Campbell, Gigi Hadid, Swizz Beatz, and Kendall Jenner. "The party was definitely interesting and tons of fun, but for us it was basically an advertising campaign."

Workshop events, van Wyck explained, are conceived thinking first and foremost about key takeaway images, and making sure that there is plenty of B-roll to create content down the line. That's why at Workshop, unlike at Van Wyck & Van Wyck, there are staff members with extensive digital, marketing, and media backgrounds. However exciting or fun, a Workshop event must satisfy the client's key performance indicators, or KPIs, to be successful.

"They give you a budget and with that you are supposed to achieve this many customer impressions, or new introductions, inquiries, or sales," van Wyck said. "Our advantage is that Workshop can draw from the history, expertise, and culture of the Van Wyck & Van Wyck team to make the actual experience amazing. Other companies may be good at digital marketing, but they have no clue about throwing a great party, so what happens is that the guests show up, they know they are supposed to tweet or Instagram, and they may do it, but the cool people don't have fun, so nothing feels authentic. It goes back to what I always say—you have to be able to make people actually *love* the brand."

The deejays, food, Halloween theme—the entire rave, in fact—were all essentially props for van Wyck's forty hand-picked influencers, whose job it was to post the content and make it go viral—which they readily did. "Afterwards there was talk in the local community about gentrification, and that created a discussion," van Wyck said. "At the same time, artists were commenting on what Lucien had done, and the supermodels generated their own little moment too—so what you ended up with was a perfect social media storm."

Johnson and van Wyck had stipulated that everyone should use the hashtag #SoBro when posting—a reference to SoHo, the well-known neighborhood in downtown Manhattan. Two weeks later, their client realized just how important the

event—and the hashtag—had been. In a piece about the evolution of the South Bronx, the *New York Times* referred to the
neighborhood as SoBro. "To my knowledge that was the first
time that had happened, and now people still refer to that area
as SoBro," van Wyck said. "At that point I knew we were at the
forefront of the industry in terms of brand-building by creating stories. We pushed the envelope in order to maximize our
client's return on investment, and I'm proud of that."

It's difficult to quantify exactly what the return on
Rubenstein's investment was, but here's a clue. "We got more
than two billion media impressions from that one night," van
Wyck said. "Rubenstein had just bought the properties for
$56 million, and he sold them in 2019 for $165 million to
another developer, without even having built the apartments.
So think about the numbers there: he spent one million on
the rave, and in some way—however you want to define it—
we contributed to the creation of that new value. That is the
Workshop objective."

There were other incentives to create Workshop. Many of
van Wyck's savvier fashion and luxury clients were well aware of
how events had evolved in the era of social media, but van Wyck
wanted to reach others who might have been lagging behind.
Having a separate company made that easier. "I was worried that

sometimes Van Wyck and Van Wyck's story was getting in the way of us being able to tell our clients' stories," he said. "If we were doing a party for Chanel, I wanted everyone to feel that Karl Lagerfeld himself had picked everything down to the very last flower. But that gets harder to do once you are well known and people are aware of what your work stands for. I was worried that we were in danger of becoming too much a part of the story."

Van Wyck also wanted to branch out from the luxury sector and was afraid that some potential new clients might find his existing roster intimidating. "Van Wyck and Van Wyck was perceived as being at the very high end—we catered to luxury clients, high-net-worth individuals, and charities. I didn't want to get hired by a bank, for instance, and have the CEO's wife ask him, who did the partners' dinner? And when he told her it was Van Wyck and Van Wyck she might say, oh my God, they're the best, but they're also the most expensive! It could create conflicts. I wanted to work with Target or the NBA, and I thought it would be best for me to become invisible for those kinds of clients—to create a company that was more of a service-driven black box operating like an agency."

Creating new opportunities for his staff was another advantage of not having his name front and center. "By then there were people who had been with me for fourteen years, and I wanted them to feel like they had a company that they could develop and own," he says. "Also, I realized that I had spent so much time building my business, but that I wouldn't be able to sell it if someone ever wanted to buy it, because I would never be able to walk away from something with my name on the door. So I wanted to build a company that I wouldn't be emotional to part with if that opportunity ever came along."

Eventually we got back to discussing what the future might look like for van Wyck and his team. He was worried that even if a treatment for Covid-19 was discovered relatively quickly, the economic devastation would be so profound by then that his business would still be in serious trouble. It could be a scenario similar to the months following the Great Recession of 2008, when celebrating had taken on a negative connotation in light of all the upheaval that was taking place.

I reminded him that, against all odds, 2008 and 2009 had actually been good years for him, and pointed out that the 1920s had been a roaring decade. Once World War I and the 1918 flu pandemic were over, people had been desperate to let loose. Hopefully, I said, a vaccine would be available soon and van Wyck would be busier than ever. Of course, there was also a chance that Covid-19 would be with us for a long period of time— maybe even indefinitely—with ebbs and flows of contagion across different populations and geographies. Too much was still unknown, and it was impossible to predict what the "new normal" that everyone kept talking about would actually look like.

The only reasonable course of action was to simultaneously prepare for both scenarios. After the pandemic eased, people would still be getting married; they would want to celebrate birthdays or special occasions. And, even during trying times, brands needed to maintain open lines of communication with their customers. Van Wyck was in touch with all of his clients to strategize as the situation evolved. Events would be more intimate for a while; possibly more of them could be outdoors. And, without a doubt, digital alternatives had to be examined more seriously than ever.

Along with everyone on the planet, van Wyck had noticed how stir crazy everyone was at home, hosting everything from cocktails to full-blown dance parties online. Even the marquee events of the season had gone digital. To virtually celebrate the Met Gala, Anna Wintour, the editor of *Vogue* and chairwoman of the event, enlisted the singer Florence Welch to perform and the designer and all-around creative powerhouse Virgil Abloh to deejay on YouTube. Simultaneously, a group of young kids hosted their own version of the gala, complete with virtual invitations and digital branding. To attend, all you needed to do was post on Twitter your look via a vision board, photograph, or collage using the hashtag #HFMetGala2020. I felt that this signaled an important shift. Instead of living vicariously through the paparazzi pictures of Lady Gaga doing multiple outfit changes on the steps of the Metropolitan Museum, or of Rihanna sashaying in a designer getup specifically conceived to break the Internet, young people were taking matters into their own hands, holding online versions of the events that they would likely never be able to attend in person.

Meanwhile, art galleries, unable to receive visitors, were organizing digital tours and creating online viewing rooms. Fairs like Art Basel Hong Kong and Frieze New York, which year after year drew hundreds of exhibitors and thousands of visitors, had moved online, too, maintaining their regular schedules. Fashion houses, most of which were already used to live-streaming their catwalk shows, were creating virtual gatherings for new launches. Music concerts, guided meditations, cooking classes, doctors' appointments, gym workouts, college graduations . . . everything was being done on two-way video. Even the city of New York had jumped into the fray, advising pent-up residents that instead of being intimate with someone who wasn't a part of their households, "video dates, sexting, or chat rooms may be options for you."

These are just a few examples of how Covid-19 accelerated the virtual interactions that have become part of everyday life over the past decade. It was clear that this trend would continue even beyond the quarantine, thanks to constant technological innovations and urgent considerations such as reducing our carbon footprint by working from home or avoiding unnecessary travel. This was already a given for a new generation of digitally savvy kids, like the ones who organized the Twitter Met Ball; in the future, they would expect to be able to choose whether to attend a party (or conference, or family reunion) either in person or virtually, and have both experiences be similarly rewarding. Anyone who had previously refused to confront the fact that we now simultaneously exist in a physical and digital realm was forced to accept this reality.

Van Wyck was considering how this might affect him. "Eventually things will snap back, but I'm already planning ahead for the next crisis," he told me when we spoke a few weeks later, still from our respective homes. "I'm developing a virtual venue for events. A client could decide, for example, that he wants to have a party at the base of the Eiffel Tower, or at the pyramids in Egypt, or in Narnia. We would virtually create that world and then the host could make choices, like hiring a deejay, or if he wants to upgrade he could have a virtual Rihanna concert. We would still be responsible for the lighting, the flowers, the rooms—it would be an environment designed with the same care and thought that our clients currently enjoy. Guests would create an avatar of themselves and put together outfits with designer clothes, interacting with others at the party."

Variations of that idea already exist, but the key consideration for van Wyck was to make sure that people would be able to communicate publicly and privately on this would-be platform. "What Zoom and others do so well is satisfy one dimension of the human need to interact and attend events," he said. "You get to see who is there and you get to be seen. But we all know that in an actual party, the real action doesn't happen in front of everyone. It's about the unexpected conversation that three people have on a couch together, or about what happens when you run into someone at the bar or on the dance floor—and you can't do that on Zoom. So that need is not being met, and I want to create a world in which it is. The technology exists on the back end but not in the delivery, in the sense that most people don't have the necessary headsets and equipment yet. But I think in five years they will."

The shift that van Wyck was alluding to is well under way. Three decades ago, being a florist was a great way to break into the event business; these days, van Wyck looks to hire people with strong visual skills who are also technologically savvy. He points out that in his early days he would verbally describe his plans to clients; a few years later, sketches and mood boards became the norm; currently, he does digital presentations with 3-D renderings. In fact, it's entirely possible that experts in spatial computing might become the event planners of the future. A step up from virtual reality and augmented reality, spatial computing seamlessly integrates the digital and natural worlds, allowing you to program an entire space instead of a flat screen. Gamers are already familiar with this technology, and billions of dollars are being invested in refining it for fields such as retail and events.

Expanding his reach in the digital arena, then, would reinforce, not replace, van Wyck's existing business. For all the uncertainty of the moment, what became clear during our conversations was that events, whatever form they might take, would never cease to take place. At the end of the day, storytelling and being able to seamlessly bring people together would still be the most important part of an event planner's job. Throughout history, get-togethers have allowed us not just to escape everyday life, but also to make friends and find conversation, romance, or even a job. It was hard to imagine that changing.

Van Wyck has managed to make a very successful business out of what he intuited from a young age: that special occasions should be treated as such. When we give a party, we are taking part in a tradition to care for each other that goes back millennia. Whether it's an intimate anniversary dinner, a gathering to decorate a Christmas tree, or a national holiday with parades all over the country, events create a sense of family and community. Our shared experiences help form and sustain the bonds that keep us together, and they give us permission to interact in a way that might not be permissible in everyday life. Simply put, celebrating is an essential part of living in society. We are hardwired with an instinctive desire to share, congregate, and commune. Van Wyck's mission is to augment and then satisfy that need, whether it's in a personal or business setting, in real life or—possibly—in a virtual sphere.

Ultimately, what makes van Wyck a master at work is his ability to facilitate meaningful interactions by creating temporary universes that are over the top but never gauche. His guests become actors in elaborate plays that last just a few hours but are not easily forgotten. You can call him an event planner, but in reality he's an aesthetics guru, a skilled social connector, and a collaborations artist. Most important of all, he is a maker of memories.

APPENDIX

——

TIPS AND ADDITIONAL READING

There is no prescribed path to becoming an event planner. Van Wyck majored in history, and on his team there are economists, creative directors, merchandisers, marketing experts, and industrial designers. One surefire way to get an early taste of the business, however, is to experiment by hosting at home with friends and family. Here are a few tips from van Wyck to make sure that any event, big or small, is a success.

I always like to greet guests at the door with a shot of tequila—nothing gets the party going like a little liquid courage.

Plan ahead to minimize stress. You want to have the most time possible with your guests, so do whatever you can in advance, like pre-mixing drinks or preparing food that won't have you running back to the kitchen all night. Consider a buffet or family-style meal. I like food that will taste great hot or cold, like fried chicken, so everything doesn't have to be served piping hot from the oven.

Keep salty snacks stocked around the room. A few of my favorites are candied bacon, homemade kettle chips, and spiced nuts. Salt makes you thirsty, and if you're thirsty you drink more, and when you drink more who knows where the night could go. . . .

Have a library in Apple Music, Spotify, or Pandora of playlists for a variety of moods. Music sets the tone for the night, and can easily put guests in your desired mindset right away.

Keep the surprises coming! This could be as simple as changing the playlist or circulating a new round of appetizers, or as exciting as organizing a special musical performance. Your guests should always be kept guessing.

One of the most important but overlooked tips is to make sure you aren't so tied up hosting that you forget to make time for your friends. It's essential to have face time with everyone attending your party since they've made the effort to come spend their evening with you. You can greet everyone at the door, pass out canapés, or make the rounds to refill drinks. While it's your job as the host to make sure that everyone enjoys themselves, this doesn't mean you shouldn't, too.

Lighting is everything. Hospitality is about making people feel good, and everyone feels better when they look their best. Lighting is both science and art, and properly illuminating each area of a party—the room, the food, the bar—is its own discrete discipline. But lighting that prioritizes the guests separates the truly great hosts from the amateurs. There is a simple Rule of Three when it comes to lighting people: three sources, from three directions, in three colors. There should be light from above, light from below, and light from the side. Overhead lighting, such as that from a chandelier, provides the foundation for all the other light in a room; gentle side lighting, from sconces, candles, or the reflected glow from a wall that's being hit from above or below, gives life to the human face; and light from below lifts and firms. Votive candles are the simplest way to light from below. They're also practically free, so I always start with more than I need and then take some away.

When setting a table, don't be afraid to combine different styles and patterns, and always mix the old with the new. Shop your home: I like to break out some family treasures since this ensures a one-of-a-kind look that's meaningful to you. For greenery, I like to have magnolia or eucalyptus garlands on the table or a mixture of blooms in a single color. You can never go wrong with white or red flowers.

There's no magic number when it comes to the guest list. Having a well-curated mix is far more important than the amount of people.

Seating can play a make-or-break role in the success of your event. You can frame an entire evening with the stroke of a pen on a place card. It's your opportunity to be both strategic and benevolent: spreading around the most interesting guests creates multiple anchors for the social energy that is essential for a great night and encourages those who are more introverted to open up and drop their reserve.

Some hosts separate married couples at the dinner table. This rule made perfect sense when marriage was a more practical— and often arranged—institution. Husbands and wives today are more likely to actually like each other, so whether or not to separate spouses becomes a consideration particular to the couple in question. It's very personal and has nothing to do with the worldliness or sophistication of the guests.

You should never stop the party when it's in full swing. Guests are always going to remember the first and last thing that happened to them, so you don't want their final impression to be of you asking them to leave. To keep people on your good side while getting them out of the house, suggest a group outing to your favorite bar, or a visit to a diner for a late-night snack. Call some Ubers to take everyone there; once they are in the cars no one will be too upset if you suddenly say you're too tired to go.

In order to avoid having the room feel empty, you absolutely need to choose a venue that matches the number of guests. If you're entertaining at home and are worried that your guest list is looking a little thin, you can make sure everyone congregates in just one room simply by closing the doors to everywhere else. If your dining room table is too big for a small dinner, make the meal a pseudo chef's table and set up seats around the island in your kitchen.

The one thing you absolutely cannot do is skimp on liquor or food. This doesn't mean that you have to buy crates and crates of that special wine you're serving with dinner. The later it gets, the cheaper the liquor you serve can be. As the night wears on, people don't really care what they're drinking as long as their cup is full. This goes for food, too. I've yet to meet someone who doesn't love a bowl of Lay's potato chips late at night.

Two foolproof ways to easily refresh the mood are to change the playlist and dim the lights. If everyone is looking a little bored, blast your favorite dance songs. And remember that people are usually afraid to misbehave under bright lights—turning them down low gives everyone permission to be naughty.

At the end of the night, don't try to clean up all at once. Blow out the candles, rinse off the dishes, and load the dishwasher. Everything else can wait until the morning. If you're moving furniture or keepsakes for ambience, always take a picture of where everything was before doing so. You'll save yourself hours of wondering if everything looks right when you put it all back.

In terms of social media, nowadays everyone is obsessed with what pops in pictures: bold colors, lots of prints. It often seems like the mantra is, the bigger and brighter, the better. But the most important thing to remember is that you want to live in the moment and experience the night itself. Don't let the pursuit of the perfect photo overtake your event. Ultimately, the conversations you have are way more important than the pictures you take.

ADDITIONAL READING:
VAN WYCK'S FAVORITE BOOKS

A Passion for Flowers, by Carolyne Roehm

Albert Pinto Orientalism, by Alberto Pinto

Alexander McQueen: Savage Beauty, by Andrew Bolton

Alexis: The Memoirs of the Baron de Redé, edited by Hugo Vickers

Area: 1983–1987, by Eric Goode and Jennifer Goode

Art of Burning Man, by N. K. Guy

Axel Vervoordt: Timeless Interiors, by Armelle Baron

Barefoot Contessa Parties! Ideas and Recipes for Easy Parties That Are Really Fun, by Ina Garten

Be My Guest, by Rena Kirdar Sindi

Blooms: Contemporary Floral Design, by Phaidon Editors

Cabana Anthology, by Martina Mondadori Sartogo

Cecil Beaton's Bright Young Things, by Robin Muir

Celerie Kemble: To Your Taste, by Celerie Kemble

Chinoiserie, by Dawn Jacobson

Death & Co: Modern Classic Cocktails, by David Kaplan and Nick Fauchald

Decorating in the French Style, by Jacques Garcia

Disco: An Encyclopedic Guide to the Cover Art of Disco Records, by
      Disco Patrick and Patrick Vogt

Dreams Through the Glass: Windows from Bergdorf Goodman, by
      Linda Fargo

Edie: American Girl, by Jean Stein

*Farm from Home: A Year of Stories, Pictures, and Recipes from a
      City Girl in the Country*, by Amanda Brooks

Feasts of Eden, by Ruby C. Thomas

Flower Color Guide, by Darroch Putnam and Michael Putnam

Great English Interiors, by David Mlinaric

Great Houses, Modern Aristocrats, by James Reginato

Hamptons Gardens, by Jack deLashmet

Hotbox: Inside Catering, the Food World's Riskiest Business, by
      Matt Lee and Ted Lee

Interiors—The Greatest Rooms of the Century, by William Norwich

Leafing Through Flowers, by Daniel OstTony Duquette*, by
      Wendy Goodman and Hutton Wilkinson

Legendary Parties: Costume Balls of the Twentieth Century, by
      Jean-Louis de Faucigny-Lucinge

*Life of the Party: The Biography of Pamela Digby Churchill
      Hayward Harriman*, by Christopher Ogden

Martha's Flowers, by Martha Stewart and Kevin Sharkey

Modern Manners: An Etiquette Book for Rude People, by P. J. O'Rourke

My Beverly Hills Kitchen: Classic Southern Cooking with a French Twist: A Cookbook, by Alex Hitz

Night Fever: Designing Club Culture 1960–Today, by multiple authors

Party of the Century: The Fabulous Story of Truman Capote and His Black and White Ball, by Deborah Davis

Peter Callahan's Party Food, by Peter Callahan

Philippe Starck, by Philippe Starck

Protocol, by Capricia Penavic Marshall

Proust's Duchess, by Caroline Weber

R.S.V.P.: Menus for Entertaining from People Who Really Know How, by Nan Kempner

Setting the Table: The Transforming Power of Hospitality in Business, by Danny Meyer

Seventies Glamour, by David Wills

Slim Aarons: Once Upon a Time, by Slim Aarons

Speakeasy: Classic Cocktails Reimagined from New York's Employees Only Bar, by Jason Kosmas and Dushan Zaric

Studio 54, by Ian Schrager

Susan Mason's Silver Service, by Susan Mason

Take Your Time, by Olafur Eliasson

The Andy Warhol Diaries, edited by Pat Hackett

The Art of the Hollywood Backdrop, by Richard M. Isackes and
Karen L. Maness

*The Art of Outdoor Living: Gardens for Entertaining Family and
Friends*, by Scott Shrader

The Art of the Party, by David Stark

The Duchess of Richmond's Ball, by David Miller

*The Duchess Who Wouldn't Sit Down: An Informal History of
Hospitality*, by Jesse Browner

The Encyclopedia of Monograms, by Leonard G. Lee

The Leopard, by Giuseppe Tomasi di Lampedusa

The Lion, the Witch and the Wardrobe, by C. S. Lewis

The NoMad Cocktail Book, by Leo Robitschek

The Odyssey, Homer, translated by Emily Wilson

The Royal Pavilion at Brighton, by John Morley

The Southerner's Handbook: A Guide to Living the Good Life, by
Garden & Gun

*The Ultimate Bar Book: The Comprehensive Guide to Over 1,000
Cocktails*, by Mittie Hellmich

The Way We Lived Then, by Dominick Dunne

United States Protocol, by Mary Mel French

Upstairs at the White House: My Life with the First Ladies, by J. B.
West

Vanity Fair's Hollywood, by Christopher Hitchens

Vogue and the Metropolitan Museum of Art Costume Institute: Parties, Exhibitions, People, by Chloé Malle and Hamish Bowles

Vogue Weddings, by Hamish Bowles

Wine Simple: A Totally Approachable Guide from a World-Class Sommelier, by Aldo Sohm

ACKNOWLEDGMENTS

Special thanks to Holly Brubach, who introduced me to the Masters at Work series, and to Stuart Roberts, my editor at Simon & Schuster.

ABOUT THE AUTHOR

Armand Limnander is the executive editor of *W* magazine. *Becoming an Event Planner* is his fourth book.